Men-at-Arms • 443

The Army of Herod the Great

Samuel Rocca • Illustrated by Christa Hook
Series editor Martin Windrow

First published in Great Britain in 2009 by Osprey Publishing
Midland House, West Way, Botley, Oxford OX2 0PH, UK
443 Park Avenue South, New York, NY 10016, USA
E-mail: info@ospreypublishing.com

© 2009 Osprey Publishing Ltd.

All rights reserved. Apart from any fair dealing for the purpose of private study, research, criticism or review, as permitted under the Copyright, Designs and Patents Act, 1988, no part of this publication may be reproduced, stored in a retrieval system, or transmitted in any form or by any means, electronic, electrical, chemical, mechanical, optical, photocopying, recording or otherwise, without the prior written permission of the copyright owner. Enquiries should be addressed to the Publishers.

A CIP catalogue record for this book is available from the British Library

ISBN 978 1 84603 206 6
ebook ISBN: 978 1 84908 121 4

Editor: Martin Windrow
Page layouts by Myriam Bell Design, France
Typeset in Helvetica Neue and ITC New Baskerville
Index by Fineline Editorial Services
Originated by PPS Grasmere, Leeds, UK
Printed in China through World Print Ltd.

09 10 11 12 13   10 9 8 7 6 5 4 3 2 1

FOR A CATALOGUE OF ALL BOOKS PUBLISHED BY OSPREY MILITARY AND AVIATION PLEASE CONTACT:

Osprey Direct, c/o Random House Distribution Center,
400 Hahn Road, Westminster, MD 21157
Email: uscustomerservice@ospreypublishing.com

Osprey Direct, The Book Service Ltd, Distribution Centre,
Colchester Road, Frating Green, Colchester, Essex, CO7 7DW
E-mail: customerservice@ospreypublishing.com

Osprey Publishing is supporting the Woodland Trust, the UK's leading Woodland conservation charity, by funding the dedication of trees.

www.ospreypublishing.com

Dedication

The book is dedicated to my children, Yair, Avigail and Daniel

Artist's note

Readers may care to note that the original paintings from which the colour plates in this book were prepared are available for private sale. All reproduction copyright whatsoever is retained by the Publishers. All enquiries should be addressed to:

Scorpio Gallery, PO Box 475, Hailsham, East Sussex BN27 2SL, UK

The Publishers regret that they can enter into no correspondence upon this matter.

THE ARMY OF HEROD THE GREAT

Presumed portrait of King Herod. In the 1960s this bust depicting a man wearing a chin-beard was found near Memphis in Egypt; dated to the Late Hellenistic period, it had been remodelled in the 3rd century AD. Although some scholars identify it with one of the later Ptolemys, others – most notably Vermeule – believe that the subject is Herod; this is quite possible, since it was found in an Idumaean context. (Courtesy Museum of Fine Arts, Boston)

INTRODUCTION & CHRONOLOGY

Herod's army was the last independent regular Jewish army before the creation of *Zahal*, the defence force of the State of Israel, some 2,000 years later. It was an army of the Classical age, and most of its features clearly show Hellenistic and Roman influences. Thus, to describe the army of King Herod is to describe a typical Hellenistic army in its last phase of development, when Roman influences were most evident. Herod's army fought for its king, but also for Rome, and in fact it is the best-known example of an army of a client king of Rome. Thanks to the books of Josephus – *War* and *Antiquities* – the activity and the organization of Herod's army have come down to us in considerable detail, despite the notorious lack of surviving pictorial evidence.

CHRONOLOGY

66–63 BC Civil war in the Hasmonaean kingdom of Israel between Hyrcanus II, supported by Antipater the Idumaean (father of Herod the Great), and Hyrcanus' brother Aristobulus II. The two brothers each appeal for help to Pompey the Great.

63 BC Pompey besieges and defeats Aristobulus II at Jerusalem. Hyrcanus II is appointed High Priest. The Hasmonaean kingdom is dismembered.

49 BC Hyrcanus II and Antipater side with Julius Caesar after his victory over Pompey at Pharsalus.

47 BC Caesar bestows on Hyrcanus II the titles of *ethnarch* and Ally of Rome, and names Antipater as *epitropos* or chief minister.

44 BC Antipater makes his sons Phasael and Herod *strategoi* in Jerusalem and Galilee. Herod executes Ezekias, a bandit leader.

44–42 BC Cassius, leader of the assassins of Caesar, rules Syria. Antipater is murdered by a certain Malichus, perhaps with the connivance of Hyrcanus II. Herod in his turn kills Malichus. After the battle of Philippi, Hyrcanus II and Herod become clients of Marcus Antonius, the new ruler of the Roman East.

40 BC The Parthians invade Roman Syria and Judaea, and set on the Judaean throne the Hasmonaean prince Mattatihu Antigonus. Hyrcanus II and Phasael, Herod's brother, are both captured;

	the first is mutilated, the second commits suicide. Herod flees first to Nabataea and then to Rome. With the support of Antony and Julius Caesar's heir, Octavian, he is proclaimed in Rome as King of Judaea.
39–37 BC	Herod reconquers the kingdom of Judaea from Mattatihu Antigonus, with the support of the Roman army of Antony and Sosius. Herod's brother Joseph is killed during the conquest of Galilee.
34 BC	Antony grants to Cleopatra the balsam plantations near Jericho, part of Herod's kingdom and an important source of income.
32 BC	First Nabataean War. Herod fights against the Nabataeans on behalf of Antony and Cleopatra and defeats them, but Cleopatra sends an army against Herod. After the battle of Actium, Herod sides with Octavian.
30 BC	At Rhodes, Herod is confirmed King of Judaea by Octavian, and is given back the territories taken by Cleopatra. Thus Herod receives Jericho, as well as the Decapolis region with the cities of Gadara and Hippos, the Samaria region, and the coastal cities of Gaza, Anthedon and Straton Tower, which had been made independent by Pompey and Galbinius.
27–25 BC	Herod sends 500 soldiers to Aelius Gallus, Prefect of Egypt, for his campaign in Arabia.
25 BC	The city of Samaria is rebuilt as Sebaste in honour of Augustus (formerly Octavian).
23–22 BC	Augustus grants Herod the territories of Trachonitis, Batanaea and Auranitis. Herod visits Octavian's military commander, Agrippa, on Lesbos.
20 BC	In Syria, Augustus grants Herod the territory of Zenodorus in Ituraea. Herod's kingdom has now achieved the same borders of the Hasmonaean kingdom at its greatest extension.
20–19 BC	Herod begins the rebuilding of the Temple.
15 BC	Agrippa visits Herod in Jerusalem. The Temple is dedicated.
14 BC	Herod and his chief minister Nicolaus of Damascus join Agrippa in Asia Minor, where he is received by the local Jewish communities. Herod's fleet takes part in Agrippa's Bosphoran war.
12 BC	Herod travels to Rome to accuse Alexander and Aristobulus, his sons by Marianne the Hasmonaean, in front of Augustus at Aquileia. Augustus temporarily settles the dispute between Herod and his sons.
10 BC	Herod travels to Rome. Dedication of Caesarea Maritima. Alexander and Aristobulus are condemned to death and executed at Sebaste. Antipas, Herod's son by his first wife Doris, is now all-powerful at Herod's court.
9 BC	Second Nabataean War. Herod is for a time in disfavour with Augustus.
7 BC	Thanks to the good offices of Nicolaus of Damascus, Herod is restored to Augustus' favour.

4 BC	Death of Herod. His kingdom is divided between three surviving sons: Archelaus is Ethnarch of Judaea, Samaria and Idumaea (4 BC–AD 6); Antipas is Tetrarch of Galilee (4 BC–AD 39); and Philip is Tetrarch of Gaulanitis, Hauranitis and Batanea (4 BC–AD 33). Unrest and military mutinies break out.
AD 6	Augustus annexes the territories of Archelaus to the Roman province of Syria. Judaea is ruled thereafter by a series of equestrian prefects, of which the best known is Pontius Pilatus.
AD 39	Agrippa I, the grandson of Herod via Aristobulus, is appointed by the Emperor Gaius Caligula as ruler of the tetrarchies of Philip and Antipas.
AD 41	The Emperor Claudius appoints Agrippa I as King of Judaea.
AD 44	Death of Agrippa I; Claudius annexes the whole of Judaea, which is ruled thereafter by a series of equestrian procurators.
AD 50	Agrippa II, son of Agrippa I, receives from Claudius the territory of Chalcis.
AD 53	Chalcis is annexed to the Roman Province of Syria; in exchange, Claudius grants Agrippa II the territories of Philip's tetrarchy (Bathanea, Trachonitis and Gaulanitis). After Claudius's death, the Emperor Nero grants to Agrippa II part of Galilee, Perea, and the cities of Tiberias and Tarichea. Agrippa II establishes his capital at Panias.
AD 44–66	The political and social situation deteriorates. Rise of the Zealots.
AD 66–70	The Romano-Jewish War. Agrippa II sides with Rome, and his small army joins that of Vespasian and Titus in quelling the rebellion. In AD 70 Jerusalem is besieged and stormed and the city and Temple are destroyed.
AD 70–94	Agrippa II rules Galilee with confirmation by the successive Flavian emperors Vespasian, Titus and Domitian. In AD 73 the fall of Masada to the governor of Judaea, Flavius Silva, brings the rebellion to an end.
AD 100	Agrippa II's death terminates not only the Herodian dynasty, but also independent Jewish rule. His territories are annexed to the Roman Empire.

HEROD AND HIS ARMY

The King of the Jews

From the middle of the 6th century BC onwards, Judaea was dominated in turn by the Achaemenids, the Ptolemys and the Seleucids. In 549 BC, Cyrus, the Achaemenid ruler of the Medians and Persians, conquered Babylonia. Cyrus then gave permission to the Jews, exiled there since the destruction of Jerusalem (including King Solomon's First Temple) in 586 BC, to return to Judaea and to rebuild the Temple. The returning Jewish exiles from Babylonia built the Second Temple, and created a small theocratic state under the leadership of a succession of high priests.

TOP **Bronze coin of Hyrcanus II (r.66–40 BC), minted at Jerusalem. It depicts on the reverse a wreath with a Paleo-Hebrew inscription 'Jehochanan the High Priest and the Council of the Jews', and on the obverse a double cornucopia symbol, adopted by the Hasmonaeans.**

BOTTOM **Bronze coin of Mattatihu Antigonus I (r.40–37 BC), bearing the double cornucopia on the obverse and on the reverse a wreath. This last Hasmonaean ruler was placed on the throne by the Parthian invasion in 40 BC, and resisted Herod's Roman-sponsored campaigns to depose him for three years.**

After Alexander the Great's conquest of the Persian Empire, the Ptolemys and then the Seleucids dominated Judaea, but each overlord granted to the Jews freedom of worship. However, in 168 BC the Seleucid ruler Antiochus IV of Syria began a programme of forced Hellenization; when he ordered the Jews to abandon the Torah, their ancestral law, and forbade circumcision, the Jews rebelled against their Seleucid overlords under the leadership of Judah the Maccabee. Four years later, in 164 BC, Judah entered Jerusalem and consecrated the Temple. He defeated the Seleucid armies in various battles – most notably the Seleucid general Nicanor, at Hadasa – but in 161 BC he was defeated and killed by the Seleucid general Bacchides at Elasa. Judah was succeeded by his brother Jonathan the Hasmonaean (r.161–143 BC). Jonathan took advantage of the civil wars then ravaging the Seleucid kingdom, earning his appointment by Alexander Balas, a Seleucid usurper, as high priest and *strategos* of Judaea.

As the new legitimate ruler of Judaea, Jonathan was nevertheless still tied to the Seleucid overlords. His brother Simon (r.143–135 BC) continued in Jonathan's footsteps, and the Seleucid ruler Demetrius II appointed him *ethnarch* of Judaea and high priest. The Seleucid yoke was only definitively thrown off by Simon's son, John Hyrcanus I (r.135–107 BC). Originally appointed *ethnarch* and high priest by the Seleucids, in the last years of his rule John Hyrcanus conquered Idumaea, parts of Galilee and Samaria. Most of the population of Idumaea converted to Judaism. John Hyrcanus's son Judah Aristobulus I (r.104–103 BC) reigned for only a year, but he styled himself as king in his own right rather than simply *ethnarch*, while continuing to rule the Jews as high priest. After his untimely death his brother, Alexander Jannaeus (r.101–76 BC), succeeded him both as king and high priest.

During Alexander Jannaeus' reign Hasmonaean Judaea became a regional power. This warlike and despotic king successfully fought against the Ptolemys, the Nabataeans, the Seleucids, and – in a vicious civil war – against his Pharisee opponents. Alexander Jannaeus conquered the coastal cities of Dora and Gaza, most of the Decapolis, and the Hauran regions in Transjordan. One of the most important courtiers of Alexander Jannaeus was a certain Antipater the Idumaean, the father of the future King Herod. On his death in 76 BC Alexander Jannaeus left the kingdom to his wife, Queen Salome Alexandra (76–66 BC), who ruled in the name of her son Hyrcanus II.

At Salome Alexandra's death civil war broke out between Hyrcanus II, supported by Antipater the Idumaean, and the king's brother Aristobulus II. The two brothers each appealed for the help of the Roman general Pompey the Great, who had an army in Syria, and in 63 BC Pompey besieged and defeated Aristobulus II at Jerusalem. Hyrcanus II was appointed high priest, although he was deprived of the royal title, and the Hasmonaean kingdom was dismembered. Judaea was dominated by Roman Syria, and after Hyrcanus II was forced to call on the Roman governor Galbinus in 57 BC to put down a revolt the country was divided into five nominally self-governing territories. Although Hyrcanus II still ruled in name at Jerusalem the real power lay with his supporter Antipater the Idumaean. In 49 BC, at Antipater's prompting, Hyrcanus II sided with Julius Caesar after Caesar defeated Pompey at the battle of Pharsalus, and Jewish soldiers helped in the Alexandrian War. In recognition, in 47 BC Caesar bestowed on Hyrcanus II the title of *ethnarch* and 'Ally of Rome'; Antipater the Idumaean was rewarded with the title of *epitropos* or chief minister. In 44 BC the all-powerful Antipater made his sons Phasael I and Herod *strategoi* or military governors in Jerusalem and Galilee; the young Herod distinguished himself, capturing and executing Ezekias, the leader of a robber band.

The Herodian kingdom included the core of Judaea, with the regions of Samaria (with a significant Gentile population), Galilee, Idumaea, and the coastal region with the exclusion of the free city of Ascalona. Octavian (Augustus) granted Herod Samaria, the Decapolis and several other previously independent cities in 30 BC, and the northern regions of Gaulanitis, Batanea, Trachonitis (which included Ituraea) and Auranitis in 23 BC.

The strict observance of the Second Comandment during the Second Temple period, forbidding the making of 'graven images', denies us Jewish figurative art from this period and thus direct evidence of the appearance of clothing and armour. In their absence we are forced to rely upon a few well-known sources of sculptural evidence for generic Hellenistic war gear from elsewhere in the contemporary Mediterranean and Middle East. One panel on the 1st-century BC 'Altar of Domitius Ahenobarbus' in Rome depicts preparations for the sacrifice of a bull during a religious ceremony, with at the left the figure of the war god Mars in the armour of a Hellenistic senior officer – an Attic helmet, a 'muscle' cuirass with *pteruges*, and greaves. (Courtesy Musée du Louvre, Paris)

However, the assassination of Julius Caesar in 44 BC embroiled Judaea in the consequent Roman civil wars. Between the years 44 and 42 BC Cassius, one of the leading assassins of Caesar, was master of Syria; and during this period Antipater the Idumaean was murdered by a certain Malichus, perhaps with the connivance of the old Hyrcanus II, who was jealous of Antipater's power. Antipater's second son Herod, with the permission of Cassius, avenged his father by killing Malichus. The rule of Cassius in the Middle East did not last for long, and after his and his fellow-assassin Brutus' defeat and death at the battle of Philippi, Hyrcanus II and the young Herod became clients of Marcus Antonius (Antony), the new ruler of the Roman east.

In 40 BC, while Antony was in Egypt in Cleopatra's arms, the Parthians invaded Roman Syria and reached Judaea, bringing with them the Hasmonaean Mattatihu Antigonus II, the son of Hyrcanus II's brother Aristobulus, who had been defeated by Pompey and taken prisoner to Rome. Antigonus II was installed by the Parthians as their puppet king in Jerusalem. The captured Hyrcanus II had his ears and nose cut off, and according to Jewish law no man with a physical deformation could hold the office of high priest. Herod's brother, Phasael I, preferred to commit suicide rather than to fall into the hands of Antigonus II. Herod's family was besieged at the desert fortress of Masada in Idumaea, and Herod, now almost alone, knew that the only possible source of real help was faraway Rome. His first stop on the journey was at Petra, the capital of the neighboring Nabataean kingdom, but he received no help there; he proceeded to Egypt, and thence to Rome. There, supported by Antony, he was appointed by the Roman Senate as King of Judaea. Over the following three years he would reconquer Judaea from the hands of Antigonus II.

The status of Herod's army

The strong bond between Herod and his army was probably the foundation of his rule. The best example is Herod's governance of Galilee, assigned to him by his father Antipater (Josephus, *AJ* XIV, 156–184, and *BJ* I, 203–216). When he returned to Jerusalem, Herod had to face the Sanhedrin – the supreme court of justice – to justify the strong-arm methods he employed to suppress local banditry. When Herod appeared in front of the Sanhedrin surrounded by his bodyguard he was immediately acquitted, but the episode did not end there. Herod had to flee from Jerusalem to Sextus Caesar, the Roman governor of Syria. There he was nominated *strategos* of all Coele-Syria. Once more, Herod returned to Jerusalem to face both the ambiguous Hyrcanus II and the Sanhedrin. Only the pleas of his father Antipater and his brother Phasael persuaded the young Herod not to take up arms against his ruler (Josephus, *AJ* XIV, 177–184) when, backed by his troops, he placed himself in opposition to the legitimate authority of the state. By his successful defiance Herod became an alternative source of authority, more successful than Hyrcanus. When Herod became king the army continued to enjoy its privileged position. It was the pillar of the Herodian state precisely because its oath of allegiance was to the king himself and not to the population. Like his model Alexander the Great and like the other Hellenistic kings before him – including the Hasmonaeans – Herod was the actual commander-in-chief of his army.

This point should be stressed particularly for another reason: that Herod's army was probably the most important force for cohesion in his kingdom. It was composed of disparate elements coming from the various ethnic populations; gathered together in its ranks were Jews (probably the majority of its soldiers), Greeks from various cities of the kingdom, as well as Ituraeans and even Nabataean mercenaries. Herod's royal bodyguard included such exotics as Celts, Germans and Thracians. His strongly charismatic personality was the common bond between all these groups of soldiers from diverse populations that would normally have had different allegiances. Thus, upon Herod's death his armed forces fall apart, and his state as well. Part of the army took an oath of allegiance to his son Archelaus and his Roman overlords, while another part of it rebelled against them, plunging Judaea into a vicious civil war (Josephus, *AJ* XVII, 206–298). The idea of an army intimately connected with and faithful to the ruler and not to the state is part of a heritage common across the Hellenistic world, and Archelaus' personality was not strong enough to hold his father's army together.

Aerial photograph of the model of Jerusalem that is today in the Israel Museum, depicting the city as it was in the last years before the great war of AD 66–70, at the end of the Second Temple period. The viewpoint is roughly south-east to north-west. (Courtesy Albatross)
(1) Herod's palace complex
(2) Herod's citadel
(3) Antonia fortress
(4) Temple Mount
(5) First Wall
(6) Second Wall
(7) Third Wall

The Herodian army was therefore an instrument of King Herod's rule, but it was also an auxiliary force for Rome, since Herod was a client king. This is reflected in its organization, which was that of a Hellenistic army with many Roman features. This was not exceptional; by the middle of the 2nd century BC the Seleucid army of Antiochus III and the Ptolemaic army of Ptolemy IV both showed Roman characteristics in their organization and in the weapons used by part of the heavy infantry. Like the armies of the Seleucids and the Ptolemys (and perhaps also of the Hasmonaeans) before him, Herod's army showed strong Roman influences. Several senior command posts were filled by Roman or Italian mercenary officers. The heavy infantry was organized according to a Roman model. The Herodian soldiers were apparently accustomed to build temporary military camps like those constructed by the Roman legions, and the military engineers were Roman-trained. Nevertheless, the king's bodyguard, the light infantry and the cavalry probably followed a Hellenistic model, and the proportion of cavalry to infantry reflected that of other Hellenistic armies. Last but not least, the Herodian military colonies also originated in Hellenistic models, as did the fortifications scattered around the kingdom.

STRENGTH & COMPOSITION

According to Shatzman, Herod's army numbered around 20,000 men at the beginning of his reign, and about 16,000 men in its last years. The problem with calculating an exact number of soldiers is that Josephus, more often than not, does not provide us with numbers of men, but only with the Greek names of certain types of military unit. Nevertheless, it is possible to estimate the number of Herod's soldiers from the different tactical units mentioned by Josephus. Thus Josephus makes mention of *ilai* to indicate units of cavalry, and of *telos* or *meros* to indicate units of light and heavy infantry respectively. These terms are also used by such Hellenistic writers as Asclepiodotus, Aelianus and Polybius to indicate Hellenistic as well as Roman units, or Hellenistic units modelled on corresponding types of Roman units.

Josephus may use the term *ile* in the Herodian context to indicate the *ile* of Aelianus, which numbered 200 men, commanded by an *ilarch*. The term *telos* is normally used by Josephus to indicate a large unit of light infantry numbering 2,000 men. However, when Josephus uses the term *telos* instead of *lochos*, he probably means an infantry unit of 512 men. Josephus uses the word *lochagos* to refer to the commander of a *telos* or light infantry unit. The meaning of his use of the term *meros* is speculative. Several Greek authors, including Polybius, use this word to indicate the Roman legion. In Josephus the term is used in the context of the Herodian army to indicate the *sebastenoi*, a heavy infantry formation probably modelled on a Roman legion, though of smaller size – only *c*.3,000 men.

It is thus possible to make an estimate of the total strength of Herod's army at three different stages: the first at the beginning of the civil war against Mattatihu Antigonus in 39–37 BC, and at its end during Herod's siege of Jerusalem in 37 BC; the second during the First Nabataean War in 32 BC; and the third at Herod's death in 4 BC.

This relief of *c*.230 BC from the Temple of Athena at Pergamon in modern Turkey depicts 'trophies' of Hellenistic armour: on the left, a sword similar to a *falcata*, and a linen cuirass with *pteruges*; and on the right, a curved scabbard and a helmet with both Thracian and Attic features. In the centre is a *scutum* shield with a pronounced strengthening 'spine' and unusual 'ear' extensions, overlaying a round Macedonian-type shield. (Courtesy Staatliche Museum, Berlin)

Strength during the civil war

It is difficult to extrapolate from Josephus the exact numbers of Herod's soldiers during his conquest of the kingdom. It seems that at the beginning of the civil war Herod's army totalled between 3,000 and 5,000 men. Josephus wrote that Herod appointed his brother Joseph to govern Idumaea with 2,400 soldiers (Josephus, *AJ* XIV, 413–414, and *BJ* I, 303). Josephus later wrote that the force sent by Herod against the robbers dwelling at Arbel in Galilee consisted of an *ile* of cavalry and three *tele* of infantry (Josephus, *AJ* XIV, 415 and *BJ* I, 305). In this case *telos* probably means *lochos;* thus on that specific occasion Herod's force amounted to 200 horsemen and *c*.1,500 light infantrymen. Forty days later Herod marched to Galilee with his entire army, which numbered *c*.3,000–5,000 men (Josephus, *AJ* XIV, 416 and *BJ* I, 305). As Herod later marched to Samaria with 3,600 soldiers, probably an equal number must have remained in Galilee (Josephus, *AJ* XIV, 431–432 and *BJ* I, 314–316). Herod also had garrisons in other places including Samaria, Joppa and Jericho (Josephus, *AJ* XIV, 411 and *BJ* I, 302). Thus, before the siege of Jerusalem in 37 BC Herod's entire force perhaps amounted to 10,000–12,000 soldiers.

It was probably only after Antony's victory over the Parthians at Gindarus that the Roman commander Ventidius could send Herod two legions – around 8,000 men – and 1,000 cavalry under the command of Machaeras (Josephus, *AJ* XIV, 434 and *BJ* I, 317). Later, Antony sent another reinforcement commanded by Sosius, consisting of two legions and other forces, to help him in the final stages of his operations and the siege of Jerusalem (Josephus, *AJ* XIV, 447 and *BJ* I, 327). In the same period Herod recruited 800 mercenaries from Mount Lebanon in Ituraea (Josephus, *AJ* XIV, 452 and *BJ* I, 329). For the siege of Jerusalem, Josephus in *Antiquities* gives Herod's total strength as 30,000 men (Josephus, *AJ* XIV, 468), perhaps including the armies of both Herod and Sosius. In *War*, however, Josephus writes that Herod's army consisted of 11 infantry units (*tele*) and 6,000 cavalry (Josephus, *BJ* I, 346). If he had intended to mean Roman soldiers he would have used the term *meros* or legion, not *telos;* moreover, it is difficult to imagine that here Josephus would have used the world *telos* with the same meaning as he previously used *lochos* – if so, the entire Herodian infantry would have amounted to no more than 5,500 men. It appears that in this case the term *telos* indicates an infantry unit numbering around 2,000, so the entire infantry numbered around 12,000 men. If we add 6,000 cavalry (although this probably also includes Roman cavalry), we arrive at a total of about 15,000 Herodian troops.

Line drawing from a Hellenistic trophy on Rhodes, depicting the typical panoply of a Hellenistic senior officer: a plumed and embossed Attic helmet, a muscled and embossed cuirass over *pteruges,* and a short sword slung from a baldric. See Plate B1.

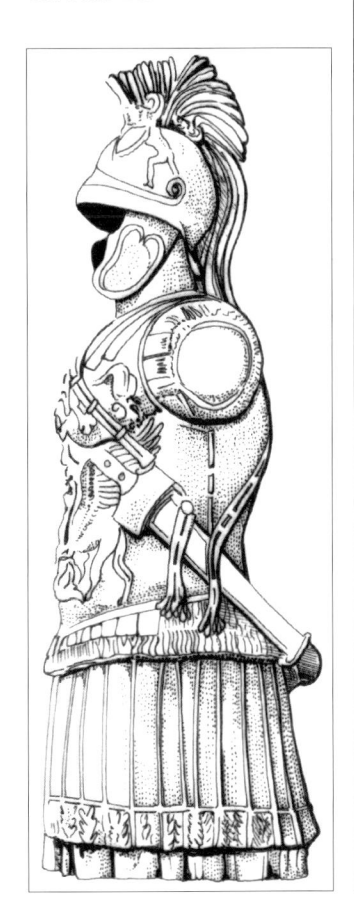

Another scene from the Altar of Domitius Ahenobarbus shows two 1st-century BC infantrymen and a horseman. All wear ringmail body armour, the left-hand man with doubled shoulder-pieces like those of a Greek linen cuirass and his comrade possibly with Celtic-style caped shoulders. The footsoldiers carry oval *scuta* shields with the spinal bar swelling out into a 'barleycorn' boss, and the cavalryman clearly wears a Boeotian helmet and has a sword at his left hip. (Courtesy Musée du Louvre, Paris)

However, the number given by Josephus probably represents only the army that Herod employed in the siege, not the additional forces left to garrison Galilee, Samaria and Idumaea, so his entire forces probably totalled *c.*25,000 men. At the beginning of the campaign Herod had sent Joseph with 2,400 soldiers to Idumaea; this figure may suggest that the number of soldiers left behind to garrison Galilee, Samaria and Idumaea was *c.*7,500–10,000. The Roman army that participated in the final phase of the civil war, including the siege of Jerusalem, numbered around another 30,000, of whom at least 12,000 would have taken part in the siege itself.

Strength in the First Nabataean War
In 32 BC Herod was sent by Antony to fight against the Nabataeans. Josephus does not report the number of Herodian soldiers, but does give the Nabataean losses in battle as initially 5,000 dead (*BJ* I, 383) and 4,000 prisoners (*AJ* XV, 157), and later another 7,000 dead (*AJ* XV, 158 and *BJ* I, 384). The total losses of the Nabataean army thus amounted to some 16,000 casualties. It is possible to suggest that the Nabataean army could have numbered no more than 30,000 men – a huge army for a kingdom without a centralized administration – since Josephus insists that the Nabataeans suffered terribly high casualties. Herod's army would probably have numbered more or less the same as their foes. We return once more to the numbers of the Herodian army after the siege of Jerusalem, around 25,000 men.

Strength at Herod's death
The size of Herod's army at the time of the rebellion following his death in 4 BC may be estimated on the basis of Josephus' descriptions. The leaderless army was divided between two factions, one following Herod's legitimate but deeply disliked heir Archelaus, the other joining the rebels. Archelaus had 3,000 soldiers who followed Herod's Roman

commanders Rufus and Gratus – probably the Sebastenoi, together with an *ile* of cavalrymen of the same formation (Josephus, *AJ* XVII, 266) – and the royal guard numbering another *c.*3,000. There was also an undetermined force probably 1,500 strong under the command of Achiab, Herod's cousin (Josephus, *AJ* XVII, 270). Thus, most of the soldiers faithful to Archelaus were from the Gentile component of the army, including its Roman commanders. The rebellious majority of the army was probably made up entirely of Jews; according to Josephus, the rebel army included no fewer than 10,000 veterans of the Herodian army (Josephus, *AJ* XVII, 270, 297 and *BJ* II, 55, 76–77). Thus, Herod's army in the last year of his reign probably numbered no more than 18,000 soldiers. To this standing army we may add *c.*13,000 military colonists – see below, 'Reserves' – whom Josephus does not mention as taking part in the rebellion, to give a grand total of *c.*30,000 men actually or potentially available.

Ethnic composition

Although scholars long argued that Herod's soldiers were for the most part foreign mercenaries, modern authorities such as Shatzman believe that the majority of his troops were in fact Jews, and that Herod's army thus did not differ much from the Hasmonaean army that preceded it. Josephus writes that during the civil war of 39–37 BC many countrymen joined Herod's army after his landing at Ptolemais (Josephus, *AJ* XIV, 394 and *BJ* I, 290). Later, after the conquest of Joppa, men from the 'local population' once more enlisted, probably Jews as well as Idumaeans (Josephus *AJ* XIV, 396–7, 400 and *BJ* II, 292–294); even Jews from Jerusalem (*AJ* XIV, 400 and *BJ* I, 294) and Jericho (*AJ* XIV, 458 and *BJ* I, 335) joined Herod's army. Jews continued to provide the majority of his soldiers even after his rise to power. Thus, during the First Nabataean War, it seems that the vast majority were Jews (Josephus, *AJ* XV, 111, 113, 115, 116, 119, 124, and 127–140 and *BJ* I, 366, 371, 373–379, 382, 384), and this is supported by Herod's speech delivered specifically to his Jewish soldiers. Lastly, describing the revolt after Herod's death, Josephus writes that most of the royal troops joined the rebels (*AJ* XVII, 266 and *BJ* II, 52); clearly these soldiers were Jews, since the Gentile mercenaries would have had no interest in joining a Jewish rebellion.

Nevertheless, many foreign mercenaries did indeed serve in Herod's army – Greeks, Ituraeans, Thracians, Gauls and others. Cilician, Pisidian and probably Thracian mercenaries had already fought in the armies of the Hasmonaeans, probably in specific units. In the Herodian army, with the exception of the Ituraeans (who fought in light infantry units), all the other foreign mercenaries were concentrated in Herod's bodyguard, which represented only a modest percentage of the total army.

Simitthus, the monumental tomb of a Numidian prince. The treatment of the surface suggests that this may depict ringmail armour modelled on the traditional Greek-Hellenistic cuirass of stiffened linen, with deep shoulder-pieces brought forward and fastened on the torso, worn over a jerkin with hanging *pteruges*. (Author's photo)

Supreme and senior command

Josephus does not give much data on the subject, but it is possible to reconstruct the command hierarchy of Herod's army. At its head, obviously, was King Herod himself. His position was not honorary; like any other Hellenistic king he personally directed operations in the field, during both the conquest of the kingdom and the First Nabataean War. Josephus characterizes Herod as having a professional attitude towards field command; he was not only competent in campaign strategy and in logistics, but also had the ability to communicate with his soldiers and arouse their military prowess, as his speech to the army during the First Nabataean War clearly shows.

The superior officers recorded by Josephus are either members of Herod's family or stem from Roman Italy. The former included the king's brother Joseph (Josephus, *AJ* XIV, 413, 438, 448–450 and *BJ* I, 323–325), sent by Herod to reconquer Idumaea from Antigonus' partisans; and his cousin Achiab (Josephus, *AJ* XV, 250, XVII, 184, 270, 297 and *BJ* I, 662, II, 55, 77) is mentioned as a commander during the civil war that followed Herod's death. It would be interesting to know if the various commands assigned to members of Herod's family, or to Idumaeans such as his kinsman Costobar (Josephus, *AJ* XV, 253–255), were reflections of talent for command or simple nepotism, since his real lieutenants appear to have been commanders of Italian, perhaps even Roman background. A certain Volumnius appears as *stratopedarch* (Josephus, *AJ* XVI, 332 and *BJ* I, 535); one Rufus was in charge of the infantry of the Sebastenoi, and Gratus commanded that unit's cavalry (Josephus, *AJ* XVII, 275–276, 283, 294 and *BJ* II, 52, 58, 63, 74). Perhaps they were also the commanders of Herod's bodyguard (Josephus, *AJ* XVII, 266 and *BJ* II, 52). These Romans may have had a double task: to organize the Herodian army on a more solid footing, and to serve as a link between the armies of Herod and of Augustus. It is not impossible that Augustus, at Herod's request, sent them to support him as 'military advisers'. However, it is also possible that these three Italians or Romans were political exiles without any connection to Augustus; perhaps they were veterans of Antony's service to whom Herod granted refuge so as to employ their military talents.

Josephus uses the vague terms *hegemones* and *strategoi* to indicate the senior officers of the Herodian army, and their exact duties are difficult to identify. In the Hellenistic world these two terms have both civil administrative and military connotations. Both were also utilized in relation to the Roman army, with reference to various duties at every echelon. The only senior officer with a specific task in the Herodian army was the *stratopedarch*, a Greek translation of the Roman legion's *praefectus castrorum*. In the Herodian army these officers of Roman origin probably always had an active role; in time of peace as well as in wartime their main task was to direct the *poliorcetica*, the construction of siege engines and artillery, and during campaigns the *stratopedarch* was also responsible for the erection of the temporary camps.

Drawing of a terracotta figurine from Myrina in modern western Turkey perhaps depicting the armour of a Galatian soldier. The raised comb of the headdress recalls that of a Thracian helmet. The muscled cuirass, with short *pteruges*, may be of metal or of hardened leather. The sword is worn on the left hip; and the oval *scutum* seems to have an added metal boss plate. King Herod is known to have employed Galatian guardsmen.

Engineers and artillery

The strong Roman strong influence on the Herodian *poliorcetica* is suggested by Josephus' description of the siege of Jerusalem in 37 BC (Josephus, *AJ* XIV, 466). Directly supervised by Herod, this was reminiscent of the siege of Alesia by Julius Caesar in 52 BC; like Caesar, Herod enclosed the city with a ring of fortifications, erected towers, and cut down all the trees around it. In creating this ring of circumvallation Herod's engineers, under the direction of the *stratopedarch*, clearly followed Roman practices in addition to the Hellenistic one of preparing siege towers and catapults. Herod's army clearly possessed artillery, both for siege work and to protect fortifications (Josephus, *BJ* V, 267, 347, 358–359 and VII, 177). Although Josephus does not state this specifically, when describing the Jewish rebels defending the walls of Jerusalem against the Romans in AD 70 he relates that they had artillery. It is probable that this artillery dated from the reigns of Herod or Agrippa I, since the rebels did not have the necessary knowledge to build these machines themselves. Although Herod's heavy infantry did not use field artillery as the Roman legions did, the textual and archaeological evidence makes clear that Herod's fortifications were armed with both arrow-throwing and stone-throwing machines. All Herod's siege works and artillery were probably organized on a Roman model.

One of the most important responsibilities of the *stratopedarch*, which shows Roman influences on the Herodian army, was probably the introduction of the Roman temporary camp or *castra*, built every day after the march by the Roman army while on campaign. Two arguments support this: firstly, Josephus' description of the First Nabataean War (*AJ* XV, 112 and *BJ* I, 367) has Herod's army erecting a military camp; and secondly, the fact that the *stratopedarch*, Volumnius, was a Roman officer. Herod thus had the expertise at his disposal, and he had good reason to follow the Roman rather than a Hellenistic model. The military camps of the Hellenistic armies were not erected routinely, like the Roman *castra*; it was a rare occurrence, probably only undertaken while facing an enemy. Neither were Hellenistic encampment perimeters well protected with trenches and stockades like those of a Roman camp, so that a surprise night attack could have fatal results. The temporary marching camps built by the Herodian army were probably similar to the pattern described by Polybius.

Herod's bodyguard

Herod's guard, according to Shatzman, numbered no fewer than 2,000 soldiers. Josephus describes various units of Herod's personal guard taking part in the king's funeral procession, including the *doryphoroi*, and a Thracian, a German and a Galatian/Celtic contingent (Josephus, *AJ* XVII, 198, and *BJ* I, 672).

It is difficult to establish the strength of the *doryphoroi*, which could have numbered anything between several hundred and several thousand men. We do not even know if this was an infantry or a cavalry unit, or if it perhaps served as infantry when on guard duties at Herod's palaces and as cavalry in the field. The term *doryphoroi* has no ethnic connotation. Whatever its size, this unit probably consisted of young men from the best families of the kingdom and distinguished veteran soldiers.

Thracian soldiers could be found in the Herodian as in nearly every other Hellenistic army (including the Hasmonaean) and later in the Roman army. They served in a variety of roles, both as infantry and cavalry.

Drawing of a well-known Celtic warrior statue from Vachères, southern France, probably 1st century BC. The very clearly depicted ringmail lorica hamata *has long doubled shoulder-pieces in the style of the earlier Greek stiffened linen cuirass; in this case it probably indicates Roman influence, as may the sword slung on the right hip. Josephus records that Herod's bodyguard included Celtic mercenaries.*

No less interesting – as well as impressive – were the Celtic contingent. These Galatians had originally formed part of Cleopatra's bodyguard, and Augustus gave this small contingent of 400 soldiers to Herod after Actium as a present (Josephus, *AJ* XV, 217.) Where did they originally come from, Galatia or Gaul? In about 278 BC Celtic tribes invaded and settled in central Anatolia (modern Turkey); later their independent kingdom, Galatia, was annexed to Rome by Augustus. Galatae or Celts from Asia Minor had served in the army of the Seleucids, and Augustus raised a Roman legion from the army of the independent kingdom of Galatia. It seems, however, that the Celts who served in the Ptolemaic army, and later in Herod's, came from Gallia (modern France).

Although we know nothing of their numbers or organization, Germanic tribesmen also served in Herod's guard. Augustus had introduced a German bodyguard (*germani corporis custodes*) into the Praetorian Guard; this unit appear to have acted as infantry while on palace duties and as cavalry in the field, and probably consisted of about *cohors* strength – *c.*500 men – divided into companies of 30 men each commanded by a *decurio*. It seems likely that Herod took Augustus' German bodyguard as his model.

THE FIELD ARMY

The cavalry

We should first attempt to establish the proportional relationship between the various arms of the Herodian army, in particular that between the infantry and the cavalry. Following a close reading of Josephus, during the civil war Herod always deployed a ratio of about 4:1 or 5:1 infantry to cavalry. Thus during the conquest of the kingdom in 38 BC Herod's brother Joseph marched into Idumaea with 2,000 infantrymen and 400 horsemen (Josephus, *AJ* XIV, 413 and *BJ* I, 303) – 80 per cent to 20 per cent. Later, Herod's force at Arbela consisted of 1,500 infantrymen and 200 cavalrymen (Josephus, *AJ* XIV, 415 and *BJ* I, 303) – 87 per cent to 13 per cent. Later, Herod proceeded to Samaria with 3,000 infantrymen and 600 horsemen, again a proportion of 5:1 (Josephus, *AJ* XIV, 431–432 and *BJ* I, 314–316). During the disturbances that followed Herod's death Rufus had at his disposal 3,000 infantrymen (according to Shatzman) and 500 cavalrymen (Josephus, *AJ* XVII, 266). This relatively high proportion of cavalry to infantry is typical of Hellenistic armies but not of the Roman army. Josephus gives a good example: Ventidius sent Machaeras to help Herod with two legions (8,000–10,000 infantry) and 1,000 cavalry (Josephus, *AJ* XIV, 434 and *BJ* I, 317) – a ratio of about 8:1 at most. If the ratios given in the various examples by Josephus reflect the total ratio in the Herodian army between infantry and cavalry, as seems likely, then Herod's infantry numbered some 20,000 and his cavalry about 5,000.

Augustan-period relief from Palmyra depicting the Palmyrene gods Aglibol, Ba'alshamin and Malikbol in armour, and presumably – given their divine status – portrayed as elite cavalrymen. This wealthy trading state in modern northern Syria must have been able to afford to armour at least its elite heavy troops. Although the *gladius* sword with four-ring anchorage is distinctively Roman, there is a Hellenistic look to the cut of the *lorica lamellata* with *pteruges*. See Plate F1. (Courtesy Musée du Louvre, Paris)

The only identified unit of Herod's cavalry is the 500-strong Zamaris' Babylonian horse, which formed the military colonies settled in Batanea (Josephus, *AJ* XVII, 24). According to Shatzman, these soldiers were light-armed horse-archers who had several favoured methods of attack. One was to release their arrows at a range of about 50 yards during a frontal charge; another was to bring the mount to a half-turn and shoot their bows while turning to ride away – the famous 'Parthian shot'. Thus, the main weapons of Zamaris' unit were the composite bow and the sword; it seems quite improbable that this unit were cataphracts and thus part of the heavy cavalry. The most interesting fact about Zamaris' horsemen is that we do not know of any other auxiliary unit of the Roman army that was armed in the Parthian manner – this unit was unique not only in Herod's army but also among the armies of Rome and her other allies. It is possible that Jews living in Babylonia performed military service for their Parthian overlords, and Babylonian Jews had already served in the Achaemenid and Seleucid armies. Thus Zamaris could have been a local aristocrat who, for motives unknown to Josephus, decided to immigrate to the Roman Empire with all his retainers.

Another cavalry unit probably consisted of mounted Ituraean archers. In this case epigraphic material related to Ituraean units in the Roman army may be useful. It is known that in the 1st century AD the roughly 500-strong *Ala I Augusta Ituraeorum* served in Pannonia Inferior as an auxiliary cavalry unit of the Roman army, and its predecessor was probably a light cavalry unit in the Herodian army.

Drawing of a terracotta figurine depicting a Scythian horse-archer, armed with the sharply recurved composite bow also used by Parthian light cavalry. This may help us to reconstruct at least the basic appearance of the unit of 'Babylonian' Jewish light horse in Herod's army led by Zamaris. See Plate F3.

The infantry

Herod's footsoldiers included both light infantry units, indicated by Josephus with the term *telos* or *lochos*, and heavy infantry, indicated by his term *meros*.

The only identified unit of light infantry are the 800 Ituraean archers from Mount Lebanon (Josephus, *AJ* XIV, 452 and *BJ* I, 329); however, there were probably also other light troops from Ituraea (Josephus, *AJ* XIV, 468 and *BJ* I, 346). Again, such units later serving as *auxilia* in the Roman army are known from epigraphic sources. Some may have been *cohortes miliariae*, suggesting a total of between 3,500 and 7,000 soldiers. These Ituraean units appear to have originated in Herod's army. Those appearing in the epigraphic record are *Cohors I Augusta Ituraeorum S* (S for 'archers') that served in Pannonia and Dacia; *Cohors I Ituraeorum* that served in Germania Superior and Dacia; *Cohors II Ituraeorum E* (E for 'part-mounted') and *Cohors III Ituraeorum* served in Egypt, and the existence of *Cohortes IV, V* and *VI Ituraeorum* may be inferred from the existence of a *Cohors VII Ituraeorum* that served in Egypt.

The Ituraean archers were both mercenaries and Gentiles; it is probable that there were other light infantry units composed of Jews, including perhaps Idumaeans. According to Shatzman, the Idumaeans who were settled in Trachonitis served as archers (Josephus *AJ* XVI, 292 and *BJ* II, 58).

Impression of a battle, from the Arch of the Julii at Glanum – Saint Rémy. While it is badly worn, the various figures can be seen to wear essentially Hellenistic armour; they are armed with both spears and swords, and carry round hoplite shields with a central arm-loop and a handgrip at the edge. (Author's photo)

The best-known unit of heavy infantry in the Herodian army was the *sebastenoi*. These troops took the side of Archelaus in the civil war that followed Herod's death. According to Josephus, who calls it *meros* or a legion, it consisted of 3,000 men, comprising both infantry and *c*.500 cavalrymen, commanded respectively by Rufus and Gratus, both officers of Italian origin (Josephus, *AJ* XVII, 266, 275–276, 283, 294 and *BJ* II, 52, 58, 63, 74). Josephus mentions that after Herod's death the various Sebastenoi units appeared as *auxilia* in the Roman Imperial army, and epigraphical data confirms Josephus' account. There was a cavalry *Ala Sebastenorum* that served in Mauretania Caesarensis, and a *Cohors I Sebastenorum M* (M for *Miliaria*, 'thousand-strong', though in fact weaker) that continued to serve in Judaea. The fact that a Cohors I is mentioned means that a Cohors II also existed, thus giving a total of nearly 2,500 soldiers – close to the 3,000 mentioned by Josephus (Josephus, *AJ* XX, 122, and *BJ* II, 236 and *Acts* 27, 1).

It is probable that there were other heavy infantry units, composed of Jews and presumably organized following a Roman model, since Josephus employs various terms that could imply this. We find in his writings the terms *chiliarchos* for *tribunus militum* (Josephus, *AJ* XIV, 229, 238, 288, 291; *BJ* I, 230, 233, 235), *taxiarchos* for *centurio* (Josephus, *BJ* I, 369, 461, 491, 673), and *speira* for *cohors* (Josephus, *AJ* XIV 410, and *BJ* I, 301) in the context of units of the Herodian army, and these may probably be identified as heavy infantry. In the last example, before the siege of Jerusalem, Josephus describes five *cohortes* made up of Romans and five made up of Jews, using the same term *speira*; this might indicate that the Jews were armed in the same way as the Romans. During the civil war that followed Herod's death, Archelaus sent a *speira* and a *chiliarchos* (Josephus, *AJ* XVII, 215–216, and *BJ* II, 11). Josephus employs this term generally for *cohortes* in the Roman army, mainly for auxiliary cohorts (*BJ* XVII, 215 and *BJ* I, 323, 324; *BJ* II, 11).

These terms are likewise used by Polybius, Asclepiodotus and in Ptolemaic papyri to indicate units of heavy infantry organized and equipped like the Roman legions. Polybius translates *tribunus* as *chiliarchos*, legion as *meros*, *cohors* as *speira*, *manipulum* as *semaia*, *centurio* as *taxiarchos*, and *centuria* as *taxis*. Asclepiodotus translates *tribunus* as *chiliarchos*, legion as *phalangarchia*, cohors as *chiliarchia*, manipulum as *syntagma*, centurio as *taxiarchos* or *hekatontarches*, and centuria as *taxis*. Ptolemaic papyri translate legion as *phalanx*, cohors as *syntaxis*, manipulum as *semeia*, centurio as *hekatontarchos*, and centuria as *hekatontarchia*.

Reserves – the military colonies

The various colonies established by Herod may have played an important role in the static defence of the kingdom. Herod founded colonies in the less secure parts of his realm, and in most cases their function was to suppress rebellion among the local populations – the only exceptions appear to have been the colonies founded in Idumaea. According to Josephus, Herod settled more than 12,000 military colonists: 3,000 Idumaeans in Trachonitis (*AJ* XVI, 285); 600 followers of Zamaris in Batanea (*AJ* XVII, 24–26); an unnumbered quantity of horsemen – probably no more than 1,000 – in Hesebon (*AJ* XV, 293–296) and Gaba (*AJ* XV, 294 and *BJ* III, 36); 6,000 colonists in Samaria (*AJ* XV, 296, and *BJ* I, 403), and 2,000 Idumaeans in Idumaea (*BJ* II, 55). Thus in the northern regions of his kingdom Herod founded colonies at Trachonitis and Batanea; in the central part, in Galilee and Samaria; and in the east and south, in Hesebonitis and Idumaea. It is noteworthy that to the best of our knowledge no colony was ever founded in Judaea proper.

The colony founded in the north-eastern part of Trachonitis with 3,000 Idumaeans was established after a rebellion by local Ituraeans (Josephus, *AJ* XVI, 271 ff). The colony was destroyed in 10–9 BC during a subsequent rebellion, but was probably re-established (*AJ* XVI, 292). The primary purpose of this colony is quite clear: to implant a community of loyal veterans who could quell any local attempts at rebellion. Herod chose Idumaeans, his kinsmen, who were clearly a loyal element. Another possible purpose of the colony was, over the long term, to foster intermarriage between Idumaeans and the local population, bringing them closer to the fold of Judaism and making the area more secure by peaceful means. These settled colonists would also have provided an example to their fellow Idumaeans, who were still nomadic, of sedentary living, thus getting to the source of the problem. The other northern colony, in Batanea, was established with 500–600 cavalry veterans, Babylonian Jews who had settled in the Herodian kingdom under their leader Zamaris. This colony, named Bathyra, probably also had a dual purpose. The loyal veterans could keep the local population in check, while also presumably guarding the northern border against nomadic incursions.

In Galilee, Herod founded the well-known colony of Gabae, to check (according to Gracey) possible insurrection on the part of the Jewish population. The colonists themselves may have been Jews; in Galilee a considerable part of the population was Gentile, and brigands were always a serious problem, so it is possible that the main purpose of the

Another detail, from the 'census' panel, of the 1st-century BC Altar of Domitius Ahenobarbus. The two infantrymen wear Montefortino-type helmets and ringmail armour; that of the left-hand man has decoration on the shoulder-piece, suggesting that it may be of leather rather than mail doubling. Note that he wears his sword on the right hip. Both men carry the familiar spined oval *scutum*. (Courtesy Musée du Louvre, Paris)

Herodian bronze coin, one of a group of four denominations minted at Samaria in 37 BC, probably before Herod's capture of Jerusalem. This one depicts on the obverse a helmet – perhaps of Attic-Beoetian type – and on the reverse a Macedonian-type round shield. It is possible that both these items of equipment were used by Herod's bodyguard troops at the beginning of his reign.

Line drawings of lamellar (top left) and ribbed scale armour (top right) found in Israel, and of riveted ringmail. All these types of defence were certainly to be seen in the ranks of Herod's army.

colony was to suppress bandits and outlaws, Jewish and Gentile alike. In Samaria, Herod distributed plots of land to 6,000 men. Again according to Gracey, the main purpose of these colonies would have been to protect Jerusalem and Judaea; however, Samaria was a separate region, and one might have expected that for that purpose Herod would have founded colonies in Judaea instead. Herod probably had the unruly Samaritans in mind rather than the Jews; he selected Gentile colonists, as settling Jews here would certainly have aggravated the existing religious tensions between Jews and Samaritans.

In the south-east, the purpose of the colony of horsemen founded in Hesebon was probably to keep the local population in check, protect Jewish settlers, and contribute to the defence of the region against the Nabataeans (Josephus, *AJ* XV, 294). In the case of the various colonies founded by Herod in Idumaea it is striking that the colonists were of the same stock as the local population – around 2,000 Idumaean veterans. Since they would hardly have been trusted to quell any local rebellions the only possible purpose of colonies in Idumaea would have been to keep the Nabataeans at bay.

Several questions concerning the Herodian military colonies remain open. Were these colonists infantrymen or cavalrymen? They would appear to have included both: Idumaeans were known in the Classical period as light infantrymen, while other elements among the colonists were cavalrymen, as, for example, those at Bathyra. Did these colonies follow a Hellenistic or a Roman model? From such data as we have, probably Hellenistic. Colonists settled on the royal domain, with the possible exception of Sebaste – but that city was not a *polis* but a royal city, erected in the royal domain. The Herodian colonies appear to have followed a clear Seleucid precedent of settling veterans together in villages.

Equipment

It is difficult to reconstruct the exact equipment of Herod's army. The main frustration is, of course, that during the Second Temple period, especially between the Maccabean uprising and the destruction of the Temple, Jews upheld the Second Commandment – the prohibition on making any graven images – quite strictly. For this reason there is no figurative Jewish art from this period; although the use of symbols was widespread, and pictures of plants and even animals can often be found, human figures are not depicted. Therefore our only possible aids in reconstructing the military equipment of the Herodian army are literary sources, archaeological finds, and – particularly – comparison with neighbouring contemporary armies from the Hellenistic East. For example, coins of Herod and Archaelaus depict shields and helmets, and it is quite probable that the types represented were indeed used by Herod's army. Such literary sources as Josephus and the 'War Scroll' – one of the Dead Sea Scrolls – are also helpful in visualizing a general image of the army's military equipment.

This certainly reflected the general trends of the Late Hellenistic period, when Roman influence was widespread. It is probable that Herod's guards units and heavy infantry and cavalry were armed with helmet, cuirass, shield, spear and sword, while light infantry were armed with bows, bow-slings, and javelins like other contemporary Late Hellenistic troop types. A coin of Archelaus depicts an Attic-Boeotian helmet, a type widespread in the Hellenistic East in the last century BC. As the helmet on this coin matches archaeological evidence from the broader region, there is no reason to presume that Herod's guards and heavy infantry did not use this type. Various types of Attic-Boeotian helmets in bronze have been found throughout the Hellenistic East; it is possible that other styles of Hellenistic helmets, such as the Attic type, were in widespread use at least among officers, as were other types. (Note, however, that the Montefortino type used by the Roman legions in this period has not been found in the Hellenistic East.)

Cuirasses, too, were probably various. There is no reason to suppose that the senior officers of the Herodian army did not use the 'muscle' cuirass, universally seen among the senior officers of the Hellenistic and Roman armies. (These cuirasses are depicted on a fresco from Pompeii called the Judgment of Solomon, but we need not read much into that, of course.) Common soldiers of the Herodian guards and heavy infantry probably used the *lorica hamata*, made of iron ringmail. By the 2nd century BC the *lorica hamata* was widespread in the neighbouring Seleucid and Ptolemaic armies, which were inspired by the armour used by the Roman Republican armies. Another source of inspiration for the use of the *lorica hamata* might logically have been the Celts who formed an independent kingdom in Galatia (modern Turkey), since it was Gallic Celts who in fact invented this type of armour. The *lorica hamata* is exactly depicted on the *c.* late 3rd-century BC reliefs of the Temple of Athena at Pergamon in modern Turkey.

Two other types of armour were widespread in the Late Hellenistic East: the *lorica squamata*, made of iron or bronze scales on a fabric backing, and the *lorica lamellata*, made of metal lames or strips laced together. Both types of body armours traced their origins to the Ancient Near East. In the Late Hellenistic period these cuirasses were worn, like the traditional Greek-Hellenistic linen cuirass, with *pteruges* or series of protective straps hanging at the belly, thighs and sometimes the upper arms, as depicted in several contemporary reliefs. Archaeological excavations from Masada brought to light parts of a *lorica squamata* that appeared to be locally manufactured.

Fine example of a characteristic Roman military grave stele of the 1st century AD, from the Rhine frontier in Germany. It commemorates one Monimus, a soldier who died aged 50 in his 16th year of service as a Roman auxiliary. He carries a composite bow and arrows, and his unit is identified as *Cohors I Ituraeorum*. There may have been a direct historical link between these units of the Roman army and the Ituraean archers who were previously recruited by Herod. (Photo courtesy Landes Museum, Mainz).

Excavation drawing of a sword found at Jericho. With an overall length of c.34in (86cm), it appears to be a Roman or Roman-style *spatha* cavalry sword. As confirmed by the Palmyrene carving on page 16 high-quality Roman weapons must have been acquired or copied across the Hellenistic East.

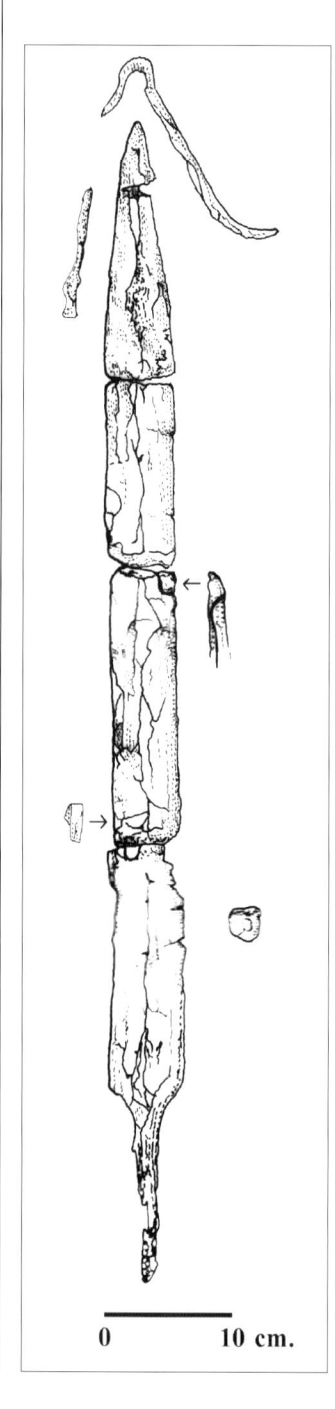

A coin of King Herod minted at Samaria in 37 BC shows a round Macedonian shield. This heavy shield was probably used by Herod's guards at least at the beginning of the reign, at least for ceremonial duties. In battle the heavy infantry would have used the early oval form of the Roman *scutum,* which is actually described in the War Scroll (in Hebrew, *magen*). Reliefs from the Temple of Athena at Pergamon, as well as a specimen found at El Fayuum in Egypt, attest the use of the oval *scutum* in the Late Hellenistic East over a broad timescale. The War Scroll describes offensive weapons such as short swords similar to the Roman *gladius* (in Hebrew, *kidon*), lances, javelins, and bow-slings. It seems that Herod's heavy cavalry used a long sword similar to the Roman *spatha,* as an archaeological find from Jericho shows. Light infantry such as the Ituraeans, and units of horse-archers, were probably armed with the composite bow. A later funerary stele, today in the Romische Museum at Cologne, depicts an Ituraean auxiliary light infantryman in Roman service armed with bow and arrows. It is probable that Herodian light infantry had neither armour nor shields.

Fortifications

Although another title by the present author is dedicated to the fortifications of Hasmonaean and Herodian Judaea, it is necessary to spend a few words on them here, since in peacetime they held garrisons of Herod's army.[1] It should be emphasized that most of Herod's fortifications were not built as protection against internal enemies; they were too powerful to have been constructed to resist either a rebellious rabble or an improbable mutiny of the army. The enemy envisaged was probably a regular army such as those of the last Ptolemys, the Parthians and the Nabataeans.

The Herodian fortifications may be divided into three main types: urban fortifications, which included city walls; the city *acropolis* and castles or *tetrapyrgia;* and smaller forts, fortlets and towers, whose purpose was to defend borders, crossroads and the countryside.

The kingdom's main cities of Jerusalem, Sebaste and Caesarea Maritima possessed walls that followed Hellenistic prototypes, although the gates and some towers were erected following Roman models. City acropolis and *tetrapyrgia* can be subdivided into two types. The first consists of citadels or fortified palaces situated inside the cities, such as the towered royal citadel and the Antonia in Jerusalem, or the acropolis of Sebaste. The purpose of these was both to defend the king during any siege of the city by an external enemy, and to protect him against possible rebellions. The second type are the fortified palaces or castles scattered all around the kingdom. Some of them were situated at important administrative centres, such as Herodium; others, such as Masada, were situated in inaccessible sites far from any urban centre. The common task of these fortifications was to protect the king, his family and his retinue.

Different regions of the Herodian kingdom each had their own particular type of administration, and each presented different challenges. Their fortifications served both to protect the surrounding area from enemies specific to that region, and as part of the general defences of the kingdom against foreign invasion. Three types can clearly be discerned: forts, fortlets and towers.

---
1 Osprey Fortress 65, *The Forts of Judaea 168 BC–AD 73*

Aerial photograph of the ruins of the upper part of Herod's fortress-palace of Herodium, built from c.23 BC. Much of the structure was 'countersunk' into a great artificial mound raised on a natural hill. (Courtesy Albatross)

Forts contained the residence of a *strategos* or military governor and occasionally, in dangerous and untamed regions, served as headquarters for the civil administration. They are structurally similar to the fortified royal palaces, albeit rather smaller. Their main purpose was administrative, but in the event of war they could also detain parts of a large enemy army. These forts were situated throughout Herod's kingdom; the best example is the *tetrapyrgion* at Horvat 'Eleq. Fortlets, generally measuring about 72ft (22m) square, were ubiquitous in Herod's kingdom. Placed along the kingdom's borders, their small garrisons could check local raids. Another task was the control of major crossroads and the protection of the local population against bandits. Finally, fortlets were built along vulnerable coastlines, both as the primary defence against hostile landings and as 'doorbells' to alert nearby forces of the standing army against such invaders.

The few excavated examples of the towers that were the smallest of the fortifications in the Herodian kingdom had the primary function of observation along routes of communication. They can be classified according to their region – Judaea, Idumaea, Galilee, Samaria, Transjordan, and the Coastal Plain and the Decapolis, where the majority of the population consisted of Gentiles who were not always friendly.

Model of the Herodian citadel, looking west to east, with the Antonia fortress and the Temple in the background. (Jerusalem Model, courtesy Holyland Hotel)

CAMPAIGNS

THE CONQUEST OF THE KINGDOM, 40–37 BC

(Our main sources for this war are Josephus, *Antiquities* XIV, 394–491, and *War* I, 290–360.)

After the Roman Senate, under pressure from Antony and Caesar Octavian, had named Herod as King of Judaea, he returned to his homeland with the ultimate end of dethroning Antigonus, the Hasmonaean ruler installed as a puppet by the Parthian invaders in 40 BC. The Parthian army had retreated back to Syria, where Antony was campaigning against them. Herod landed at Ptolemais, an independent *polis* allied to the Romans, and there he began to organize his army. It seems that his priorities were to secure Galilee, the northern part of the kingdom, and then to liberate his family besieged at Masada, and to conquer Jerusalem by a rapid surprise stroke. With an army that already included a majority of Jews, Herod marched into Galilee against Antigonus' forces there, who could only shut themselves up in strongholds and prepare for siege. Antigonus was familiar with the proverbial Roman greed, and tried, with varying degrees of success, to corrupt the Roman officers sent by Antony to help Herod. These included Ventidius, governor of Syria, and one Silo, who proved amenable to bribery.

Ventidius' priority was to settle the various disturbances caused by the Parthian invasion in the Greek cities previously settled by Pompey and Galbinius; the support of these cities, traditionally hostile to the Hasmonaeans, would be an important element in final victory. It seems, however, that throughout the campaign Herod was understandably more interested in securing the support of the Jewish population than that of the Gentile cities. Herod's policy seems to

Drawings of a silver coin minted by Caius Sosius in Cilicia in 38 BC. The following year Sosius' Roman army assisted Herod in the final siege of Jerusalem that doomed Mattatihu Antigonus and placed Herod securely on the throne of Judaea.

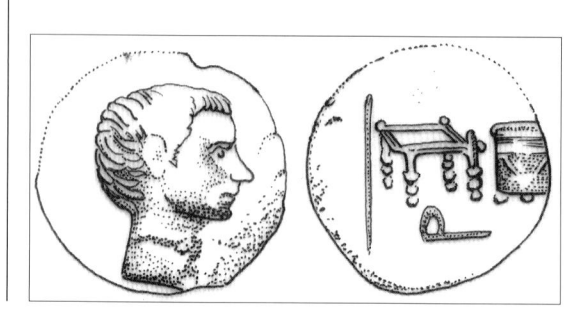

(continued on page 33)

THE WAR AGAINST MATTATIHU ANTIGONUS, 39 BC
1: Ituraean light infantry archer
2: Jewish *theurophoros*
3: Roman legionary

HERODIUM
1: King Herod as military commander
2: Jewish heavy infantryman
3: Zamaris, commander of 'Babylonian' cavalry

HEROD AND THE TEMPLE
1: King Herod
2: Herodian Galatian guardsman
3: The High Priest
4: Lower ranking priest

THE PALACE
1: Herodian 'Celtic' guardsman
2: Hatran envoy
3: Hatran bodyguard

THE IDUMAEAN HEARTLAND
1: Jewish *doryphoros*
2: *Sebastenos* armoured infantryman
3: Idumaean infantry archer

HERODIAN CAVALRY
1: Jewish heavy cavalryman
2: Thracian mercenary cavalryman
3: 'Babylonian' light cavalryman

THE ARABIAN FRONTIER
1: Herodian auxiliary cavalryman
2: Nabataean frontier guard
3: Arab tribesman

INTERNAL TENSIONS
1: *Sebastenos cavalryman*
2: *Jewish Zealot*
3: *Syrian woman*

have been widely successful in Galilee, although the garrison of the city of Sepphoris was still loyal to Antigonus. The latter begun to organize guerrilla groups to hinder Herod's army and make his conquest of Galilee insecure – a strategy that was successful until the last year of the war.

Anxious to march into the deep south to relieve his family besieged at Masada, Herod was forced to give priority to Joppa, the most important maritime city of the kingdom (meanwhile the Roman commander Silo, pursued by Jews, was saved by a providential intervention of Herod's army). Herod took Joppa without difficulty, and then relieved Masada. Subsequently his army marched for Jerusalem, unresisted except by guerrilla ambushes; he took the fortress of Ressa, and pitched his camps in front of Jerusalem.

Herod's hope of capturing Jerusalem rapidly were frustrated. The corrupt Silo's troops were in a state of near-mutiny over the lack of proper food and of winter quarters, and to calm this dangerous unrest among the Roman units and to deny Silo an excuse to abandon the siege Herod brought provisions from Samaria. Antigonus' soldiers, essentially guerrillas, had some success in ambushing Roman troops also sent to gather provisions in the area around Jericho. Herod marched to that city with ten cohorts of heavy infantry (half made up of Jews and half of Romans) some light infantry mercenaries and cavalry, but on their arrival the Romans plundered Jericho – which did not endear Herod to the local population. Herod left a garrison in Jericho, while the Roman army was billeted in various winter quarters in Judaea, Galilee and Samaria. The bribes of Antigonus now succeeded where his guerrilla army had failed: Herod was obliged to abandon the siege of Jerusalem – and with it any hope that the war would be a brief one – since Silo, once more corrupted by Antigonus, would not move from his winter quarters at Lydda. The first year thus concluded with Herod apparently dominating Galilee (with the exception of its most important strongholds), Samaria and Judaea, but with Jerusalem still in the hands of Antigonus, who used the winter respite to reorganize.

Unable to strike at Jerusalem in spring of 39 BC, Herod sent his brother Joseph south to conquer Idumaea with a force of 2,000 infantrymen and 400 horsemen. The Idumaeans were kinsmen of Herod, and it seems that their tribal loyalty justified the token size of this force, but Herod anyway had little choice. If he had taken Jerusalem the whole country would have surrendered to him, but now he had to conquer it region by region. Herod established his base in Gentile Samaria, from where he directed operations against various strongholds in Galilee, and Sepphoris, the most important, soon fell to him. Although the regular forces of Antigonus ceased to exist in Galilee after this defeat, his cause continued to be served there by various guerrilla forces, and by straightforward bandits, who were an eternal plague in Galilee.

Aerial photograph of the ruins of Masada, seen from the north. Stepped down the narrow 'prow' in the foreground is the impressive Northern or 'Hanging Palace', separated from the other buildings by a large complex of storehouses. At the right is the Western Palace, beyond the remains of the Roman siege ramp of AD 73. In 40 BC, in the face of the Parthian invasion, Herod installed his close family and some 800 guards on this boat-shaped natural clifftop, rising some 1,200ft above the shores of the Dead Sea in Herod's ancestral region of Idumaea. To guard himself against Cleopatra's expansionist ambitions several years later Herod greatly strengthened its defences and enlarged its storage of water and food to withstand a long siege. (Courtesy Albatross)

Two more examples of the Samarian-minted coin set of 37 BC. Samaria was a Gentile city, which may explain why pagan motifs are found on all four denominations minted there. In 28 BC Herod refounded the city as Sebaste; it was from this district that he recruited the Sebastenoi, one of the most important formations of his royal troops.
TOP **Here the obverse depicts the *pileum* or headdress of the *dioscuri*, while the reverse shows a tripod.**
BOTTOM **The obverse shows the cadduceus, and the reverse a poppy flower, both symbols that can be connected with the Gentile city of Samaria.**

Counter-insurgency in Galilee, 39–38 BC

To fight them Herod sent an *ile* of cavalry and three *telos* of light infantry against their nest at Arbela. The modestly-sized engagement that followed was serious enough that Herod himself had to join his army and intervene in the fighting; the Herodian left wing almost gave way, but Herod's intervention rallied his men and the enemy fled, pursued as far as the River Jordan that divided Herod's kingdom from Nabataea.

Once more in Judaea, Herod had his brother Pheroras supply the Roman troops of Silo while he himself rebuilt the Alexandrium fortress. The war in Galilee grumbled on, with the guerrillas and brigands emerging periodically from their impregnable caves to disrupt communications between Herod's forces in Samaria and Idumaea. It is recorded that Herod carried out a daring operation against these bandit lairs, having soldiers lowered from clifftops in timber 'chests' on iron chains until they could reach the cave mouths. Before launching assaults he had heralds proclaim lenient terms for surrender, and most of the brigands gave themselves up. Leaving his general Ptolemy to garrison Galilee and root out the last bandits, Herod then went to Samaria with 600 cavalry and 3,000 infantry; but Ptolemy failed to control the situation and was himself killed, obliging Herod to return to Galilee to destroy the remaining rebel strongholds.

Antony sent Herod two legions and 1,000 cavalry, led by Machaeras, but this officer too proved susceptible to bribery by Antigonus. Herod reacted by offering him an even larger bribe, but he could have no confidence in Machaeras as an active partner in the continuation of the war, so he sent him to garrison Emmaus. There Machaeras's soldiers commited indiscriminate atrocities, jeopardizing Herod's popularity; the king threatened to send the general back to Antony in disgrace, as more of an impediment than an asset, but eventually despatched Machaeras to reinforce Joseph in Idumea, far from the theatre of active operations. While Herod was visiting Antony at his siege of Samosata in Syria – where he was promised another reinforcement of two legions, under Sosius – the situation deteriorated rapidly. Joseph was killed in an ambush in Judaea, together with most of one Jewish and five Roman cohorts. This success inspired renewed uprisings in both Judaea and Galilee, and other Herodian commanders were killed. Machaeras had to fortify Gittha in Samaria, near the border with Judaea, and Antigonus' guerrillas ravaged the countryside.

Once more Herod faced the same situation as in the previous year; his conquests in Galilee and Judaea had brought no lasting result. Returning from Syria with Roman reinforcements, he also enrolled 800 Ituraean archers from Mount Lebanon – troops more suitable for guerrilla-fighting than heavy infantry. At Ptolemais Herod prepared his combined Jewish-Roman army for a decisive campaign; marching into Galilee, he attacked and captured a major stronghold, and after two years of counter-insurgency operations Galilee was finally conquered.

The siege of Jerusalem, 37 BC

When Herod subsequently marched to Jericho, Antigonus had no choice but to send out his regular army to face him in pitched battle. Antigonus struck on two fronts; in the south he sent 6,000 soldiers against the Romans encamped at Jericho, and in the north he sent his main army under his general Pappus against Machaeras in Samaria. Antigonus' troops were defeated on both fronts, and Herod himself took the offensive against Pappus. A pitched battle between their forces at the village of Isanas soon degenerated into confused street-fighting, but it seems that Herod's relatively lenient policy towards the local population bore fruit. After Herod's victory Antigonos was finally shut up in Jerusalem, and Herod once more pitched camp outside the city. Just as two years previously, winter brought active military operations to a close.

In the spring of 37 BC Herod began the siege-works, erecting triple lines of circumvallation. With the coming of the spring the main Roman army under Sosius also arrived at Jerusalem; Herod had a force of 30,000 of his own men, and Sosius 11 legions, 6,000 cavalry and 6,000 auxiliaries from Syria. The city's First Wall was taken in 40 days, the Second Wall in only 15 days. Then the Outer Court of the Temple was captured, leaving the defenders holding out in only the Inner Court and the Upper City. After fruitless negotiations Herod launched the final assault, but when the last redoubts fell the Roman soldiers behaved with a lack of restraint that led Herod to complain to Antony. Antigonus, captured by Sosius, was sent to Antony and subsequently beheaded.

In achieving the conquest of Judaea the two greatest obstacles that Herod faced had been bribery and guerrilla resistance. He overcame the first by the only possible means – bigger bribes – and the second, in large measure, by a sensible policy of relative leniency towards local populations, which is emphasized more than once by Josephus. Consequently few of the locals sheltered the guerrillas, with the valuable result that the fighting against them was kept largely outside villages and urban areas. Moreover, Herod's willingness to take a firm stance against excesses by his Roman allies also earned him popularity among many of his subjects.

THE FIRST NABATAEAN WAR, 32–31 BC

(For sources for this war see Josephus, *Antiquities* XV, 108–160, and *War* I, 364–385.)

At the beginning of the civil war between Antony and Caesar Octavian, Herod offered his army as an auxiliary force to Antony. For political reasons – mainly that Antony was unwilling to gainsay Cleopatra – he send the Herodian army against the Nabataeans. Cleopatra, queen of Ptolemaic Egypt, was disturbed that the Nabataeans did not pay tribute to her throne, and that they dominated the 'Spice Road'. For Cleopatra, sending Herod's army away from the main theatre of war had the added advantage that it would deny him any claim on the fruits of final victory; he may have been her lover Antony's client, but she was determined to expand Egyptian power at his expense.

Silver *denarius* minted by Marcus Antonius, depicting on the obverse a warship and on the reverse the standard of *Legio II*. Although Antony had been a sponsor of Herod's client relationship with Rome, he was unwilling or unable to control his lover Cleopatra's implacable enmity towards the Judaean king. Antony allowed the Egyptian queen to take from Herod wealthy territories on the coast and around Jericho; and in 32 BC, when Herod was sent by Antony – at Cleopatra's wish – to fight against the Nabataeans, Cleopatra was so alarmed by Herod's victories that she sent an army against him under Athenion. After Cleopatra and Antony were defeated at Actium by Octavian and Agrippa, at Rhodes in 30 BC Octavian restored to Herod all the territories lost to Cleopatra.

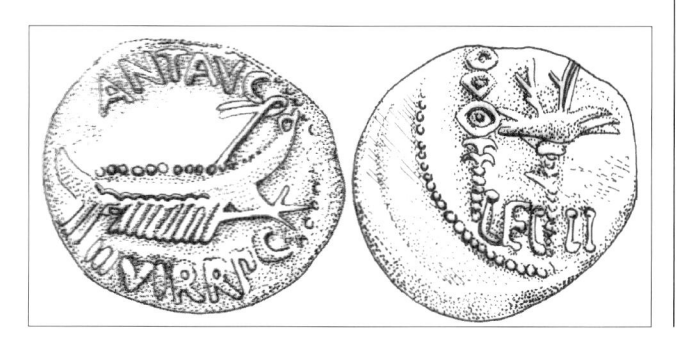

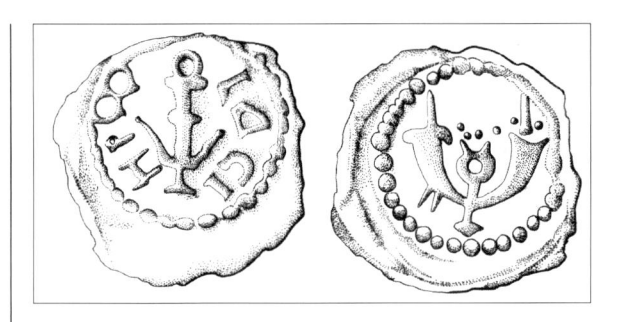

Herodian bronze coin minted at Jerusalem, bearing two motifs adopted earlier by the Hasmonaean dynasty and both taken over by King Herod in order to stress the continuity of his rule. The obverse depicts an anchor and the reverse the double cornucopia; in our colour plates we have chosen (entirely speculatively) to reconstruct both these motifs as shield blazons.

This coin depicts on the obverse a tripod, symbolic of the Temple that Herod began to renovate on a grand scale in c.20–19 BC, and on the reverse a diadem with the Greek letter *Chi* inset. This stood for *Christos* or 'Anointed', indicating that Herod was anointed King of the Jews following a coronation ceremony similar to those of the Israelite kings. Both sides of the coin thus bore symbols of his legitimacy as ruler.

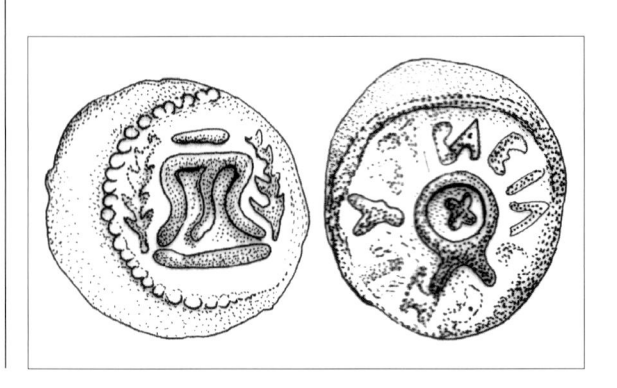

Josephus emphasizes that Herod was able to raise a strong army because the country was fertile and prosperous and thus he could levy more taxes. It is probable that five years of peace had healed the worst wounds of the war against Antigonus, and that from the beginning the idea of a war against the Nabataeans was popular – it seems that the population wanted to take revenge for Nabataean meddling in the quarrel between Hyrcanus II and Aristobulus that had brought down 20 years of civil wars upon the Jews. Herod himself was probably attracted by the chance to share with Cleopatra and Antony the future domination of the Spice Road.

Herod's primary objective was the total destruction of the Nabataean army. After he had organized his army he marched to Diospolis, where he engaged a Nabataean force. This first pitched battle between the Nabataeans and the Jews ended in a victory for Herod. The Nabataeans reorganized and assembled another army at Canatha, a city situated in the northern part of the Decapolis; Herod encamped his own army – probably in the Roman fashion – not very far from there. The enthusiasm of his army after their first victory prompted Herod to make a surprise strike against the nearby Nabataean force. (Made careless by overconfidence, Herod's army did not obey his order to erect a *castra* defended by a stockade – evidence of an insubordination that would later have dire consequences.) Once more the Nabataeans were soundly defeated. It is interesting to note that their army was composed mainly of cavalry and a camel corps, and that both their infantry and cavalry were light troops, all thoroughly familiar with the terrain on which they fought. Herod's army, on the other hand, was a more modern force composed of light and heavy infantry and cavalry. It is probable that these two battles were both mainly clashes of cavalry, in which Herod's heavier cavalry probably smashed their lighter opponents easily even before his infantry could intervene.

Cleopatra's treachery

Cleopatra, jealous of Herod's success that could jeopardize her dream of dominating the Spice Road, now sent an army against him under the command of Athenion. Herod's army, tired and probably weakened by significant casualties after two battles, now had to face a fresh enemy. The Ptolemaic army, probably larger than the Herodian, consisted not only of light troops like the Nabataeans but also had heavy infantry. It seems that Athenion's only weak point was that he did not have any cavalry; however, he ambushed the Herodians in a site where they could not use the advantage derived from their mounted strength. The Nabataeans also profited from the situation to join in the attack when Herod's army began to retreat. They attacked part of it in a camp that had been left undefended by stockades, and since this proved untenable it had to be abandoned.

However, despite this setback Herod's army did not retreat all the way to the borders of his kingdom, and it seems that Cleopatra recalled

Looking across 1st-century AD Jerusalem roughly from north to south, this shows on the right the Antonia fortress incorporated into the north-west corner of the Temple Mount. Herod completely redesigned and greatly strenghtened the original Hasmonean fortress on this site. One of its purposes was maintain surveillance of the Temple precincts, potentially a nest of sedition. (Jerusalem Model, courtesy Holyland Hotel)

Athenion's army soon after the battle. The main reason was probably the disastrous naval defeat of Actium on 2 September 31 BC: the last Ptolemaic queen had to abandon her dreams of expansion to concentrate on the urgent defence of her kingdom against the army of Caesar Octavian. After suffering such a serious defeat himself Herod had to avoid pitched battles, but his army were not idle; they sprung a number of successful ambushes on the Nabataeans, and slowly began to regain dominance over the enemy-held terrain.

Herod's reorganization of his army was hindered not only by the Nabataeans but by nature itself, since a devastating earthquake struck Judaea. After this disaster Herod wanted to cease hostilities and get back to his kingdom, so he sent ambassadors to propose to the Nabataeans terms that would probably have restored the *status quo ante bellum*. However, it takes two sides to make peace, and Herod's plans necessarily changed when the Nabataeans murdered these Jewish envoys – in the Classical world the murder of ambassadors was the worst crime a nation could commit. Nevertheless, the army was naturally demoralized by news of the consequences of the earthquake on their families, and King Herod had to encourage his soldiers with a dramatic speech. It seems to have worked: the Herodian army attacked the enemy successfully on the west bank of the Jordan, crossed the river, and pitched camp near the Nabataean army at Philadelphia in the southern region of the Decapolis.

Herod sent a detachment to capture a series of fortifications that stood between his army and the enemy, while having the defences of his own camp strengthened. After a Nabataean detachment was defeated and fell back the main Nabataean army came out from their encampment to give battle. Although more numerous than the Jews the Nabataean army was still composed of light troops; it was defeated in hand-to-hand fighting, and suffered great slaughter during its flight from the field. Trying to avoid complete annihilation, the Nabataeans then sent ambassadors to Herod in their turn, but the king refused to receive them. In the course of successive engagements 5,000 Nabataeans were killed while retreating and 4,000 were taken prisoner, and another 7,000 fell while trying in vain to hold back Herod's subsequent attack on their camp.

Herod's army had achieved all its objectives. The Nabataean army was completely destroyed, and the Nabataeans had to cede to Herod various territories and the control of part of the Spice Road; they probably also had to divert to Herod the tribute that they had been supposed to pay to Cleopatra. Moreover, Herod had achieved an even more important success. Although he had fought against the Nabataeans as an ally of Antony, he had not fought directly against Octavian (as was his duty as Antony's ally and *cliens*), and could appear in a more positive light when he faced the victor of Actium. This diplomatic success would have far more important consequences than the war itself; as the ally of the future Emperor Augustus, Herod would receive much greater territories than he had conquered with the sword.

AELIUS GALLUS' ARABIAN EXPEDITION, 25 BC

(For the Herodian army's participation in this campaign, see Josephus, *Antiquities* XV, 317, and Strabo, *Geography* XVI, 4, 22–24. Although Josephus does mention that Herod sent 500 picked men to Aelius Gallus he gives no account of the expedition, for which we must rely upon Strabo.)

The purposes of the expedition were several. After Rome's conquest of Egypt her next logical step would have been to dominate the Arabian Peninsula, and to conquer the areas where many of the raw materials of the monumentally lucrative spice trade were produced – 'to win over the Arabs, or to subjugate them'. Arabia also lay between Egypt and far-off India, thus any possible commercial relationship with India depended upon routes passing through Arabia. The Nabataeans, who dominated access to Arabia from the north, were apparently amenable, and the Nabataean *epitropos* Syllaeus promised to guide and supply Gallus' army on the march. Herod had good reasons to contribute an auxiliary unit: firstly, as a Roman client king he had no choice, and secondly it might later give him a chance of sharing in Roman profits from the spice lands. According to Strabo, Syllaeus actually wanted to dominate Arabia for himself, but the motive for his treachery – which in the end condemned the expedition to failure – was more prosaic. It is clear that the Nabataeans had no interest in any Roman domination of the spice lands, which would have been the final blow to their control of the Spice Road after Herod's victories in 32–31 BC.

Gallus prepared the expedition with care. He built 80 ships – biremes and triremes – and light boats at Cleopatris, and in addition to the warships another 130 transport vessels. His army numbered about 10,000 men, of whom 8,500 (about two legions) were Romans, 1,000 Nabataeans and 500 Jews. The Jews were picked light cavalrymen who could scout and fight in desert conditions. From Cleopatris, Gallus arrived at Leuke Kome where he spent the winter, but scurvy and fatigue were already weakening his army. Syllaeus deliberately guided the Romans through roadless country by circuitous routes, and through desolate regions far from the coast – or, if near the coast, in places where shallows and rocks hampered their resupply by the fleet. Gallus marched through Nabataea and Ararene, where the Romans fought against King Sabos, not far from the city of Negrana. According to Strabo, 10,000

Another of Herod's bronze coins bears on the obverse an eagle and on the reverse a single curnucopia. A monumental eagle is said to have decorated the façade of the Temple, and the single cornucopia – like the double motif – was a symbol adopted by Herod from the Hasmonaeans.

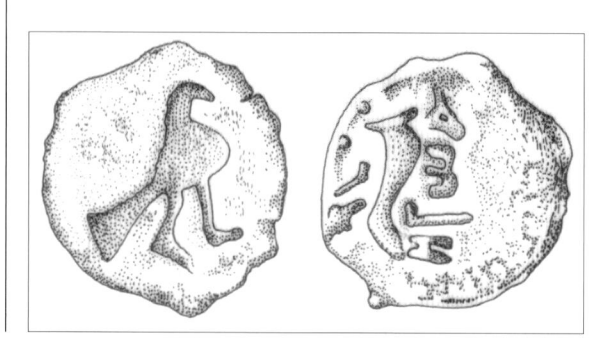

natives were killed for just two Roman casualties; however unlikely the figures, Strabo reports that the natives' only weapons were bows, spears, slings and double-edged axes, and – facing two Roman legions, even if reduced, and various auxilary cavalry – they had no chance. After the battle Gallus' army captured and garrisoned first the city of Asca and then Athrula. Thus further reduced, from there the expedition proceeded to besiege the city of Marsiaba that belonged to the Rhammanitae tribe ruled by King Ilasarus. The Romans were now only two days' distant from the 'aromatic country' – but it had taken Aelius Gallus six months to march from Leuke Kome to Marsiaba. The effective strength of his army had been reduced by perhaps half, his supply lines were overextended, and – duped by Syllaeus – Gallus did not even know that he was so near his objective.

Discouraged, he turned back. The army returned to Negrana, then to Heptha Phreata, and the villages of Challa and Malotha; the next waystation, Egra, was in Nabataean territory. The journey back took Gallus only 60 days; clearly, once the Romans gave up on their ambitious objectives Syllaeus wanted them out of Arabia as soon as possible. Hardly surprisingly for a Roman chronicler, Strabo was convinced that Gallus would have subjugated all of Arabia but for the treason of Syllaeus (Strabo, *Geography* XVII, 1, 53). Aelius Gallus' reputation was ruined, but the Arabian petty kings preferred a treaty of friendship with Rome to risking a new expedition. Herod's soldiers had aquitted themselves well. Syllaeus' treachery would be discovered only 15 years later, during the Second Nabataean War.

THE SECOND NABATAEAN WAR, 9 BC

(See Josephus, *Antiquities* XVI, 271–299, 333–355, and *War* I, 574–577.)

The Second Nabataean War stands out as one of those wars that reversed Clausewitz's principle that war is the continuation of diplomacy by other means. Although his army achieved some success, Herod first lost and later won this campaign in the diplomatic field.

The main catalyst for the conflict was once more Syllaeus' wish to destabilize Herod's power and regain, by either force of arms or diplomacy, the territories conquered by the Jewish king in the First Nabataean War. With memories of the Aelius Gallus expedition, Syllaeus also wanted at all costs to regain complete domination of the Spice Road. However, even 20 years after their annihilation by Herod the Nabataeans probably still had no army to speak of, so Syllaeus had to rely on diplomacy to regain what had been taken from him by force. Josephus adds that Syllaeus was also angry with Herod for personal reasons, since his request for Herod's sister Salome in marriage had been refused.

The occasion was given by a local rebellion in Trachonitis, which Syllaeus supported and financed. According to Josephus, the natives did not like to plough the land and to pay the taxes to their new master Herod; today we would say that these nomads had obvious difficulty in adapting themselves to sedentary life. It was probably easy to convince Syllaeus that the Nabataeans should help their fellow nomads' uprising. The rebellion was timed to coincide with Herod's absence far away in Rome, and though his generals quickly succeeded in quelling the rebels their ringleaders managed to escape to take refuge in Nabataea. This created a delicate situation for Herod. The ringleaders were not political martyrs but common brigands; with the blessing of Syllaeus they began to raid into

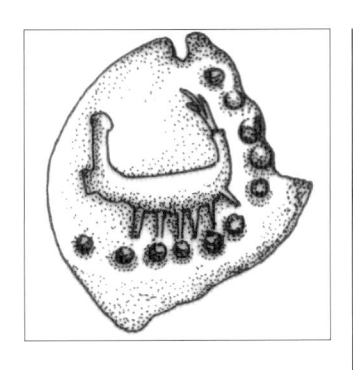

The obverse of this Herodian bronze coin depicts a war galley; it was probably minted to celebrate the foundation in 23 BC of Caesarea Maritima, renowned for its harbour.

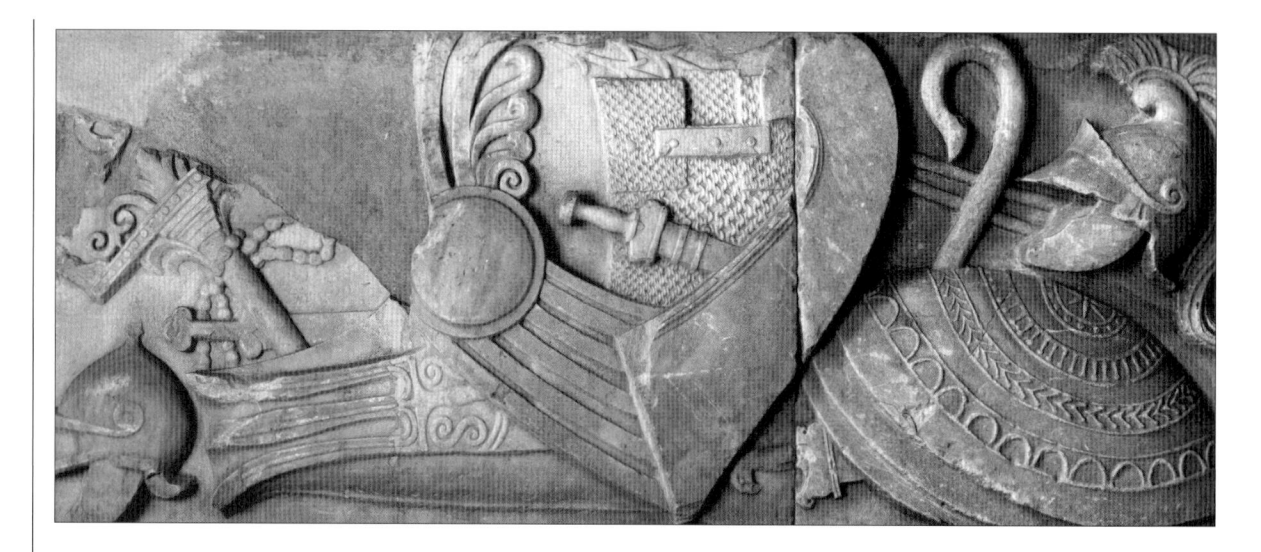

Another marble relief from Pergamon, depicting victory trophies of Hellenistic military equipment. At bottom left is an Attic Boeotian helmet, and at right a Thracian helmet above a stack of Macedonian shields. Between the symbols of a ship's stern and prow (centre) are a *lorica hamata* with a bar-latch for the shoulder-pieces, and a straight sword. (Courtesy Staatliche Museum, Berlin)

both Herod's kingdom and Roman Syria, and the number of their followers gradually increased to about 1,000 men. Syllaeus wanted to demonstrate to Augustus that Herod was incapable of maintaining his rule; meanwhile Herod had his hands tied, since to send even a small expedition into Nabataea to kill or capture the robbers would have given Syllaeus the pretext he sought for a war that would anger Rome.

Herod went to Saturninus, governor of Syria (r.10–6 BC), but made the mistake of asking him not for help in finding a possible diplomatic solution, but for his support in case of war. Herod also sought repayment of a loan of 60 talents that he had made to Obodas, the senile King of Nabataea in whose name Syllaeus wielded actual power; he therefore demanded that both the cash and the robbers be delivered up to him, under threat of war. The Roman procurator in Syria supported Herod's claim, but Syllaeus was shrewd enough to refuse. Herod now had no choice; he probably called up his reserves in case there was a major confrontation, but actually sent only a limited force into Nabataea for a local retaliatory raid, with the approval of Saturninus. The Roman governor well understood that only a determined punitive operation could restore quiet in Trachonitis and Syria. Herod besieged and captured a robber fortress at Raepta, but despite his efforts to avoid escalation fighting continued, and in another limited action a Nabataean commander named Naceb and 20 of his soldiers were killed.

Syllaeus used the death of Naceb as his excuse to go to Rome and complain to Augustus, naturally painting a very different picture of the facts and accusing Herod of mustering a 'huge' army for a war of aggression. Remarkably, given the emperor's normal shrewdness, Syllaeus seems to have duped Augustus into a hasty reaction before consulting his man on the spot Saturninus. The emperor wrote to Herod angrily, accusing him of launching an unjust war against another ally of Rome. Thus although Herod had won on the battlefield he was defeated diplomatically, and he had attracted Augustus' wrath for a more fundamental reason. In declaring war and mustering his army without the emperor's direct permission Herod had shown disrespect to the *maiestas* of Rome, giving an impression of carelessness of Augustus' authority. If Augustus was seen to have no power over Herod, his most faithful ally, then he would be weakened in the eyes of others, both clients and enemies.

However, Augustus' angry reaction did not bring any positive result or restore peace. Encouraged by the rebuke to Herod, the robbers of Trachonitis massacred most of the Idumaean colonists sent by Herod to guard the area, and for fear of further provoking Augustus Herod could not react decisively. One is tempted to wonder what Saturninus in Syria made of his emperor's hasty and unhelpful intervention in affairs on the borders of his province. However, luck proved to be on Herod's side, presenting him with a very unlikely ally. When the old king Obodas died and was succeeded by his heir Aretas IV, the new young king was suspicious that the all-powerful minister Syllaeus had designs on the throne himself. Having secured the backing of Sohemus, a rival to Syllaeus, Aretas sent to Augustus a certain Phabatus, once a steward of Herod who had been corrupted by Syllaeus but who had since been bought back by Herod. Aretas' ambassadors also carried a letter in which their king accused Syllaeus of bribing one of Herod's Arabian bodyguards to kill him, and of having killed old King Obodas with poison (which was probably true).

Despite these charges Augustus remained unconvinced, until Herod sent to Rome his last hope, his faithful Nicolaus of Damascus. Supported by King Aretas' Nabataean ambassadors, Nicolaus delivered a masterpiece of oratory and produced documents that fully justified Herod's actions. Most tellingly, he emphasized that this limited punitive raid – not a full-scale invasion – had the full approval of the governor of Syria, Saturninus. (It is possible, however, that what really changed Augustus' mind was other evidence of Syllaeus' part in the failure of Gallus' Arabian expedition. This appears in neither Josephus nor Strabo, but Nicolaus could have learned of it from either Herod's veterans of the expedition or from Aretas' Nabataean ambassadors.) At all events, the outcome was happy for Herod; he was restored to favour, and Syllaeus was beheaded for treason.

THE ARMY AFTER HEROD

The might of Herod's army dwindled away shortly after their king's death in 4 BC. Herod's death and Archelaus' succession were followed by civil disturbances and mutinies. As described above, when bereft of its commander-in-chief the army divided into two camps, one that followed Archelaus – Herod's legitimate heir, but deeply disliked by most of his subjects – and the other that joined the rebels. After the revolt was quelled by Varus, the Roman governor of Syria, Herod's army was for the most part disbanded. Part, mostly Gentiles, continued to serve Archelaus, and later on would be found as the provincial *auxilia* of Judaea. (As mentioned above, under 'The Field Army – Infantry', these included several Ituraean light infantry units; there were at least seven *cohortes* as well as the Sebastenoi, who were organized in an *ala* of cavalry and two infantry *cohortes*.) Other elements of Herod's army probably continued to serve Archelaus' brothers Antipas and Philip. Herod's reliable client army would soon be missed by Augustus and later by Tiberius. These emperors continued to send reinforcements to the East, both to replace Herod's field army and also to have units ready to put down Jewish uprisings in the destabilized aftermath of Herod's death.

The Gentile component of Herod's army was not the only element that later served Rome. Herod's eventual successors, Agrippa I and Agrippa II, mustered a small army, probably consisting of a Jewish majority and modelled on contemporary Roman practices. In AD 66 most of King

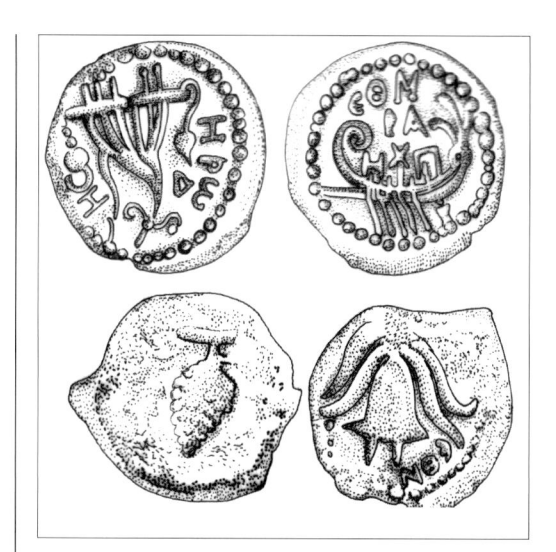

Agrippa II's army stood by the king, as an ally of Rome, against the rebels. These troops took part in the various military operations against the Jewish revolutionary government from AD 66 to 70, side by side with the army of Vespasian and Titus. Until Agrippa II died in about AD 93/94 a small army guaranteed the independence of his territories, which included Galilee and such northern regions of Herod's kingdom as Gaulanitis and Batanea. With Agrippa II's death part of his territories were annexed to the Province of Syria, and Galilee to the Province of Judaea, by the Emperor Trajan. With the death of this last Herodian ruler the last vestiges of Jewish independence disappeared for nearly 20 centuries.

Two bronze coins minted by Herod's successor Archelaus.
ABOVE **The motifs are the double cornucopia and, on the reverse, a war galley.**
BELOW **a bunch of grapes on the obverse, and an Attic-Boeotian helmet.**

SELECT BIBLIOGRAPHY

Bahat, D., *The Illustrated Atlas of Jerusalem* (Jerusalem, 1990)
Bar-Kochva, B., *Judah Maccabaeus – The Jewish Struggle against the Seleucids* (Cambridge, 1989)
Connolly, P., *The Roman Army* (London, 1976)
Connolly, P., *Hannibal and the Enemies of Rome* (London, 1978)
Connolly, P., *The Greek Armies* (London, 1977)
Connolly, P., *Living in the Time of Jesus Christ* (Oxford, 1983)
Dar, S., *Landscape and Pattern. An Archaeological Survey of Samaria, 800 BCE–636 CE* (Debevoise, NC, 1986)
Foerster, G., *Masada V, The Yigael Yadin Excavations 1963–1965, Final Reports, Art and Architecture* (Jerusalem, 1991)
Gichon, M., 'Idumaea and the Herodian Limes', in *IEJ* 17, pp.27–42
Gracey, H.M., 'The Armies of the Judaean Client Kings', in *The Defence of the Roman and Byzantine East* (Oxford, BAR, 1986)
Holum, K.G., *King's Herod's Dream, Caesarea on the Sea* (New York, 1988)
Marsden, E.W., *Greek and Roman Artillery, Historical Development* (Oxford, 1969)
Netzer, E., *Greater Herodium, Qedem* 13 (Jerusalem, 1981)
Netzer, E., *Masada III, The Yigael Yadin Excavations 1963–1965, Final Reports, The Buildings, Stratigraphy and Architecture* (Jerusalem, 1991)
Netzer, E., *The Palaces of the Hasmoneans and Herod the Great* (Mainz, 1999)
Richardson, P., *Herod, King of the Jews and Friend of the Romans* (Columbia, SC, 1996)
Schalit, A., *König Herodes, Der Mann und sein Werk* (1969)
Schürer, E., *The History of the Jewish People in the Age of Jesus Christ (175 BCE–AD 135) I* (Edinburgh, 1973)
Sekunda, N., 'Hellenistic Warfare', in Hackett, J. (ed.), *Warfare in the Ancient World* (New York, 1989) pp.130-135.
Sekunda, N., *The Seleucid Army* (Stockport, 1994)
Sekunda, N., *The Ptolemaic Army* (Stockport, 1994)
Shatzman, I., 'The Armies of the Hasmonaeans and Herod', in *Texte und Studien zum Antiken Judentum 25* (Tübingen, 1991)
Tsafrir, Y., & Magen, Y., 'The Desert Fortresses of Judaea in the Second Temple Period', in *The Jerusalem Cathedra* 2 (1982) pp.120–145

PLATE COMMENTARIES

(Additional material by David Nicolle, PhD)

A: THE WAR AGAINST MATTATIHU ANTIGONUS, 39 BC

The campaign in Gallilee involved a variety of troops drawn from various sources; it can thus be seen as a typical operation for the very mixed Herodian army.

A1: Ituraean light infantry archer

Ituraea lay immediately south-east of Mount Hermon and today straddles the front line between Syria and the Israeli-occupied Golan Heights. Its archers were renowned from ancient until medieval times, and – being a largely Gentile area – Ituraea provides several illustrative sources dating from around the time of the Herodian dynasty. The archer shown here wears a costume typical of southern Syria at this period, which was much the same whatever an individual's religious affiliation. His bow is of typical Middle Eastern composite construction, and arrows – still usually with bronze heads at this date – are carried flights-uppermost in a tubular leather quiver. In this reconstruction his right hand has been given a leather patch of a type normally associated with Persian archers, which reduced the discomfort to palm and fingers when fully drawing a powerful and relatively short bow.

A2: Jewish *theurophoros*

This 'half-light infantryman' highlights the strong Hellenistic Greek influence upon Jewish soldiers, especially of the armoured elite. His bronze helmet is of Attic-Boeotian form. His slightly convex oval shield, covered with painted parchment, has a narrow bronze rim and an iron boss covering the iron handgrip; here it almost hides a short sword with a horn hilt, carried from a baldric in a leather scabbard having numerous small bronze rivets down both edges. He is also armed with a thrusting spear and two javelins. We have reconstructed a fringed woollen cloak bearing Jewish 'notched-L' motifs.

A3: Roman legionary

One of the soldiers sent by Antony to assist Herod's conquest of his country is armoured and armed in the style of the late Republican-early Imperial decades. His bronze Montefortino helmet has a small neckguard, large hinged cheek-pieces, and a black horsehair plume; it is secured by a chin thong uniting the cheekguards and passing round his neck. His ringmail cuirass has a second layer over his upper back and extending forwards as flaps over the shoulders; the leather *pteruges* or pendant straps over his upper arms provide extra protection from cuts. A leather belt with rivetted bronze plates supports a bronze-hilted dagger in a bronze sheath on the left side and – hidden here – a *gladius* shortsword on the right. The early oval *scutum* shield has a bronze boss plate over a swollen wooden strengthening spine, and bronze binding. He is also armed with a light and a heavy *pilum* javelin with long iron foreshafts.

B: HERODIUM

The king was an enthusiastic builder who left a larger number of impressive military and civilian monuments than might be expected of the ruler of a small and relatively short-lived state on the fringes of the Roman Empire. Few were more striking than the palace-fortress at Herodium in Judaea, built on and countersunk into a huge artifical mound in *c*.23 BC.

B1: King Herod as military commander

His magnificent dress and military equipment demonstrate his role as a Hellenistic ruler in the mold of Alexander and his Macedonian Greek successors. A gilded bronze Attic-style helmet is decorated with embossed winged horses, ostrich feathers and a white horsehair crest. Beneath a mantle of deep purple with a gold fringe his gilded bronze 'muscle cuirass', hinged down one side and buckled at the other, is also decorated with winged horses; the white leather *pteruges* have gold edging and fringes. Gilded bronze greaves are held in place only by the springiness of the thin metal, and are worn above soft red leather boots. His sword, with an ivory-covered hilt, is carried in a red leather scabbard with gilded bronze edges and mounts, from a decorated red and gold baldric. The king's horse has equally magnificent harness, largely of red leather with gilded bronze studs, linkage covers, buckles and bit; the leather-covered saddle is padded but unframed.

B2: Jewish heavy infantryman

He too is equipped in essentially Hellenistic style, his bronze helmet being of Thracian shape. His tunic, as usual, is open down both sides and is decorated with two vertical stripes in a contrasting colour. The sleeveless ringmail cuirass, typical of the period – and seen as far afield as Celtic Gaul and parts of Iraq – has leather-bound shoulder flaps joined on the chest by a bronze linkage bar; the *pteruges* at the upper arm are plain leather. His short sword slung to the left hip is obscured here by his large, parchment-covered 'plywood' shield. This has two stiffening ridges around the circumference and a central spine swelling out into an iron-faced boss; narrow bronze guttering protects the top and bottom edges only from sword cuts. The speculative blazon is reconstructed from a Herodian coin showing an anchor motif.

B3: Zamaris, commander of 'Babylonian' cavalry

Whether Herod's regiment of horse-archers recruited from the large Jewish community in what is now Iraq continued to wear essentially Parthian or Iranian costume is unknown, but their military role would have ensured that their equipment remained 'Eastern'. The brightly coloured, semi-stiff felt cap given to Zamaris in this reconstruction would almost certainly have been worn over a helmet. The small horsehair plume was probably mounted on this, and the two ribbons on each side

Drawings of two Late Hellenistic Thracian helmets, both now in the Staatliche Museum, Berlin. The left example was found at Melos in Greece, the right at Prodromi.

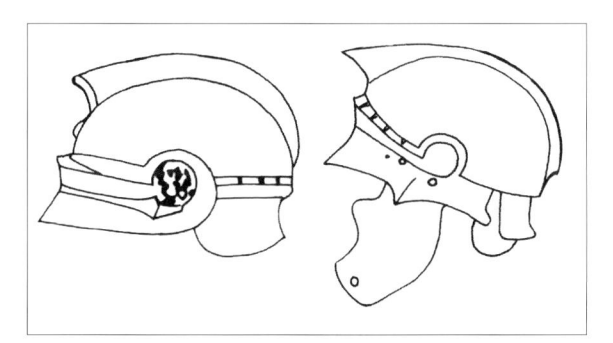

presumably tightened the cap over the helmet; a mail aventail was attached, and is tied by leather thongs beneath his chin. Shoulder defences of overlapping iron lames end in flaps with triangular ribbed scales, probably to cover straps and buckles beneath. The cap-sleeves and body of the cuirass are again made of downwards-overlapping ribbed iron scales, and have leather edging strips. A plain leather waist belt and a narrower sword belt have bronze buckles. The baggy woollen leggings are not full trousers (see also D2), and hang over soft, loose-fitting leather riding boots. He carries, unstrung, a large composite bow with stiff bone ears. The saddle and harness have relatively little decoration; the girth passes over the latter, which is of the four-horned type soon adopted by the Romans. Once believed to be of Celtic Western European origin, it is now thought to have originated in Iran. Hidden here on the right rear side of the saddle would be a leather quiver laced to a bowcase (see F3).

C: HEROD AND THE TEMPLE

Of the Second Temple, massively renovated by King Herod from c.20 BC and destroyed by the Romans in AD 70, only the vast masonry platform and the southern part of the western wall survives – the 'Wailing Wall', probably the most sacred site in Judaism.

C1: King Herod

The king's facial appearance is based on a carving found in Egypt which has been tentatively identified as a portrait of Herod the Great. Although by birth an Idumaean, stemming from a tribal Edomite people who inhabited southern Palestine and converted to Judaism just over a hundred years BC, Herod ruled almost more as a Hellenistic king than a Jewish one. Here he wears the typical attire of a successor to Alexander the Great, with a gold diadem around his head, and a fine quality short-sleeved white tunic with two vertical purple stripes and others around the ends of the sleeves. His heavy woollen mantle is again dyed in royal purple and is decorated at the corners with charcteristic 'notched-L' shapes. Inside his sandals soft leather leggings are similarly stained purple.

C2: Herodian Galatian guardsman

King Herod is known to have recruited a guard unit of apparently Celtic origins; these may have been Galatians from what is now western Turkey, or Gauls from what is now France. The soldier reconstructed here is dressed and equipped as a Galatian. He has a bronze Thracian-style helmet, a bronze muscle cuirass, and two rows of short, plain leather *pteruges* from a jerkin worn under the cuirass. His long Celtic-style iron sword has a bronze guard and pommel and a leather-covered grip; it is carried in a bronze-mounted plain leather scabbard from a baldric to his left hip. The oval shield is strengthened by a bronze rim and a bronze boss over a stiffening-bar running the whole height of the shield. The red tunic, boots and mantle have been reconstructed as suitably handsome for a palace guard unit.

C3: The High Priest

Priests are among the few public figures in Herodian times who are known to have worn a distinctively Jewish form of costume, and the attire of the High Priest in Jerusalem can be reconstructed with some confidence. Over his white linen cap is a thickly padded blue additional cap with a gold band on the brow. A blue robe, with gold thread tassels alternating around

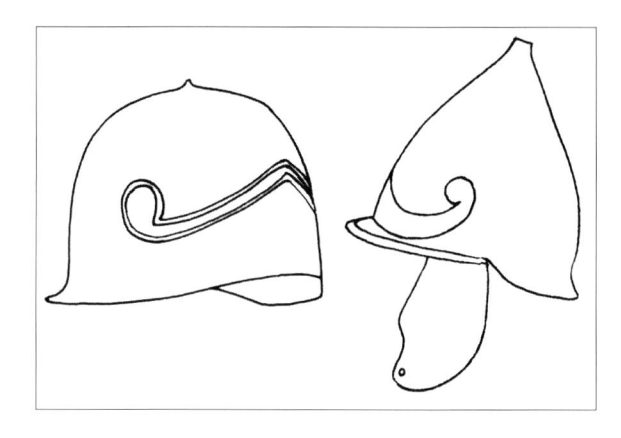

(Left) Drawing of Late Hellenistic Attic helmet found at Pergamon, Turkey, and today in the Staatliche Museum, Berlin. (Right) Late Hellenistic Attic-Boeotian helmet found at Achtanizovskaja Staniza; see Plate H1.

the hem with tiny bells and golden miniature pomegranates, is worn over a long, sleeved white linen robe. A small cape is embroidered in bands of gold, purple, scarlet and blue, with two gold shoulder-brooches inset with sardonix; from these hangs a gold purse inset with 12 precious stones. Overall is tied a long, multi-coloured girdle-cord with tasselled ends.

C4: Lower ranking priest

These are understood to have worn the same white linen caps and long-sleeved white linen clothing as the High Priest, again with a long multi-coloured girdle-cord tied many times around the body and hanging down the front.

D: THE PALACE

The Herodian kingdom was just one of several small independent (or at least, autonomous) states located between the great power-centres of the Mediterranean Sea and the Iranian plateau; all struggled to survive by using political skills and trading wealth as well as their own rather limited military means. One of this mosaic of small political entities was Hatra, a northern Mesopotamian city-state in what is now north-western Iraq; here we imagine a visiting ambassador being received at one of Herod's palaces.

D1: Herodian Celtic guardsman

Whether any of the Celtic soldiers who fought for the Jewish kingdom actually came from Gaul is unclear, and still less is it known whether any of them would have used their native Western European military equipment. The figure reconstructed here assumes that some of the most recent recruits did so. He wears a southern Celtic form of iron helmet with large cheek-pieces, and displays a large gold torque around his neck. His woollen cloak is secured by paired gold brooches, and he wears typical loose-fitting woollen trousers which tuck inside his soft leather ankle-shoes. The sleeveless ringmail *lorica* again has leather edging around the doubled shoulder flaps, which are this time attached on the chest by large iron rivets and a leather strap or thong. In addition to a plain leather waist belt with an iron buckle, to distribute some of the weight of the mail from the shoulders to the hips, the guardsman has a Gallic-style sword belt formed of an iron chain whose links consist of large rings twisted into paired smaller rings. Gaul's wealth in iron is reflected in the iron-covered scabbard of his long straight sword with an iron guard and pommel. The parchment-covered wooden shield also has an iron boss plate; the speculative blazon is taken from the double-cornucopia motif found on many Herodian coins.

D2: Hatran envoy

The visiting dignitary wears a tall quilted cap that became typical of his homeland, though it was originally of Parthian-Iranian origin. The embroidered bands that decorate his tunic were again a local example of a widespread fashion, but his very baggy trousers are ultimately Iranian or even Central Asian. So too are the heavy woollen leggings, with broad embroidered bands, which are attached to the hem of his tunic by gilt bronze 'suspenders'; like the loose riding boots, these are primarily designed for the comfort of horsemen. His leather sword belt is fastened by a large gilded bronze button through one of the several slits in the end of the belt; it passes through a bronze slide on the outer face of the sword scabbard.

D3: Hatran bodyguard

Artistic and archaeological evidence indicates that the armies of several of these minor Middle Eastern states drew upon both Mediterranean and Iranian military traditions. This elite soldier has a tall bronze helmet of early Thracian style, and a lamellar cuirass. The body is made of narrow rows of bronze lamellae, each row separated by a strip of leather. The shoulder-pieces are of similar construction, edged with leather, with bronze rosettes where they are laced down to the cuirass beneath; they seem to have bronze edging scales as well as leather *pteruges*. Below a broad embroidered band round the hem of the cuirass are three rows of *pteruges* with some gilded decoration and coloured woollen fringes. Below his green tunic baggy woollen trousers are tucked into soft leather riding boots. His plain leather sword belt supports a bronze-edged and -mounted leather scabbard; like his master's, his weapon has a bronze pommel and guard and a leather-covered grip.

E: THE IDUMAEAN HEARTLAND

Idumaea – or Edom, as it was known in ancient Biblical times – lay immediately south of Judaea, and King Herod's great fortress-palace of Masada, overlooking the Dead Sea, stood virtually on the borders of Judaea and Idumaea. The Idumaeans themselves clearly provided loyal troops for Herod, but after the fall of the Herodian-Idumaean dynasty the area and its people fell into obscurity. (Nevertheless, some scholars have suggested that the 6th–7th century AD Arab or Arabized tribe of Banu Judham who lived in this region were descended from the earlier Idumaeans.)

E1: Jewish *doryphoros*

Once again, the more professional troops from Idumaea would have been equipped in an essentially Hellenistic style. This *doryphoros* armoured infantryman has a ringmail *lorica hamata*, with additional shoulder-pieces edged in leather and attached by bronze linkages between what resemble large decorated bronze rivets. The leather *pteruges* from his under-armour jerkin have simple tooled decoration and red woollen fringes. The bronze 'muscle' greaves are secured by red leather straps. The magnificent silvered bronze shield in the Macedonian style would almost certainly have had a leather guige to support its weight on the heavy infantryman's shoulders and neck. He carries a Thracian-style bronze helmet.

Marble relief of trophies of Hellenistic equipment from Pergamon. (Top right) a *lorica hamata* with doubled shoulder pieces; **(left & centre)** a Macedonian-type shield with a running wolf blazon, over a spined oval *scutum* – note the latter's riveted rectangular metal boss-plate with three-point edge. (Courtesy Staatliche Museum, Berlin)

E2: *Sebastenos* armoured infantryman

This soldier seen from the rear has a different bronze helmet known as an Attic Boeotian style, with a horsehair plume. His *lorica hamata, pteruges* and greaves are essentially similar to E1's gear. He is armed with a long wooden spear with an iron blade and butt-spike, and protected by a *scutum* shield; note the horizontal wooden handgrip within the iron boss. Such shields were made of multiple thin wooden strips glued together in crossways layers in an ancient form of plywood, covered with parchment, painted, and protected from cuts to the edge by narrow bronze guttering.

E3: Idumaean infantry archer

Idumaea – like so much of Bilad al-Sham, 'the Land of the Semites' or 'greater Syria' – was renowned for its skilled bowmen. They were particularly effective in the broken, hilly terrain characteristic of this part of the Middle East. Few had much armour, and their weaponry was often limited. We imagine this man, however, as associated with the Masada garrison; he has a bronze helmet with a horsehair crest, his good-quality tunic has a colourful example of the type of striped decoration that seems to have been almost universal throughout the region, and his open-toed boots are of fine whitened leather. His round, parchment-covered shield has a painted edge but no bronze rim.

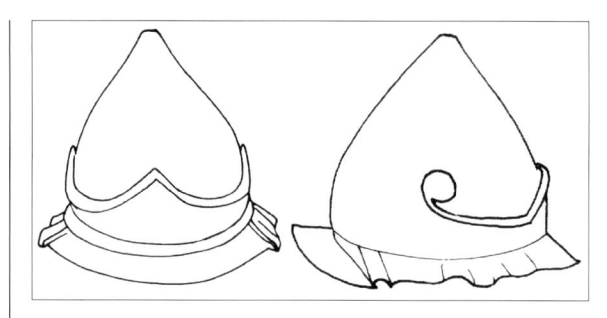

Front and side drawings of a Late Hellenistic Boeotian helmet, now part of the collections of the Ashmolean Museum, Oxford.

F: HERODIAN CAVALRY
In this reconstruction a trooper from the Herodian army's elite cavalry is showing the carvings at Qasr al-Abd to a Thracian mercenary, when a member of the 'Babylonian' unit commanded by Zamaris rides up, apparently with urgent news.

F1: Jewish heavy cavalryman
Here an elaborate form of bronze Attic-Boeotian helmet is worn, with cheek-pieces and a comb holding a red horsehair crest; just visible below the back is a gold necklace. The basic iron lamellar cuirass has additional upper back and shoulder flaps covered with brightly coloured, thickly embroidered fabric, which also covers the lowest row of lamellae at the waist (compare with D3). A bright sash is wound several times around the waist and tied in front. The springy bronze muscle greaves are additionally secured with knotted red leather straps. His slightly convex shield has a bronze rim; its decorative blazon is interpreted here as green branches and a yellow domed structure or crown. His mount (far left) has a saddle of the four-horned type, the bronze horn-plates covered with padded leather for comfort. An additional relatively loose breeching strap is tied to a ring on the breast strap; the rest of the harness has bronze fitments, and a bronze bit with bar-shaped *psalions*.

F2: Thracian mercenary cavalryman
He has been reconstructed wearing the hooded mantle that appears on various Thracian monuments. It is worn over a very loose-fitting, short-hemmed tunic with mid-length sleeves, with the comfortably baggy trousers typical of a horse-oriented culture tucked into his ankle-boots (the row of holes above the toes may be for ventilation). A leather belt with a gilded bronze buckle and strap end, hidden beneath the bloused belly of his tunic, supports a long sword with a gilded bronze hilt. He is also armed with a heavy javelin with a barbed blade. While his horse harness is obscured at this angle, he would sit a simple leather-covered but unframed saddle; just visible is the gilded bronze bit, distinctive in having the lower ends of its *psalion* bars much longer than the upper ends.

F3: 'Babylonian' light cavalryman
As in the case of Herod's Celtic troops, it is not certain that the men recruited for Zamaris' unit continued to use the traditional cavalry equipment of their homeland, but we have reconstructed this trooper as doing so. He wears the characteristic Parthian or Iranian quilted hat and a long-sleeved quilted coat; the latter was slit from hem to hips at the sides for comfort when riding. Over this is worn an additional 'overcoat' with some fur trim, or even a fur lining. The leather of his belt is almost completely faced with bronze plates, while the open D-shaped strap ends are fastened together with laces. A separate sword belt has bronze buckle, buckle plate and strap end; the long, straight leather sword scabbard, almost hidden at this angle, might have the surface almost covered with cross-strapping, a bronze chape and edging. Behind his right leg a tubular quiver and a bowcase for two unstrung composite bows are tied together and to the rear of the padded, four-horned saddle. A broad tooled-leather crupper strap has a very large bronze linkage cover, while the broad breast strap splits into two before reaching the saddle. The bronze bit has very long *psalion* bars.

G: THE ARABIAN FRONTIER
Herod's dealings with his eastern neighbours, the Nabataeans of what is now southern Jordan and north-western Saudi Arabia, were always tense and sometimes belligerent. Other nomadic Arab tribes sometimes allied themselves to one side or the other.

G1: Herodian auxiliary cavalryman
This horseman, employed to watch the ill-defined semi-desert frontier between Judaean and Nabataean territory, has limited military equipment. Unarmoured, he wears the usual open-sided tunic over a basic loincloth; his simple woollen mantle is fastened with a bronze brooch and decorated here with the 'notched-bar' motif widely popular in this period. A plain leather baldric supports a short sword with an all-bronze hilt, in a plain scabbard with bronze mounts and edging. His other weapons are a light and a heavy javelin both with iron blades. Although his harness is rudimentary the bridle is decorated with bronze studs.

G2: Nabataean frontier guard
Nabataean costume appears to have been less influenced by Parthian or Iranian styles than was that of the other great Arab trading state to the north, Palmyra, and it had several features that would survive well into early Islamic times; the same is true of Nabataean military equipment. This camel-rider is armed with a parchment-covered composite bow and a back quiver of bronze-headed arrows. Although the camel's harness appears almost agelessly traditional it in fact makes use of the recently developed northern Arabian wood-framed saddle. This made the camel a much more effective military mount and, according to some scholars, may have influenced the development of the wood-framed horse-saddle. Hanging from the saddle here are a sword with a bronze pommel and guard in a leather scabbard with a bronze slide and circular chape; a long leather quiver for three light javelins, points down; and, over sturdy goat-hair camel bags, a small leather shield with a domed bronze boss and a pair of coloured, tasseled cords.

G3: Arab tribesman
The little that is known about the costume and weaponry of the poorer bedouin tribes suggests that both were rudimentary. This man's garment is in fact an ancient version of the simple, one-piece *izar* wrap that is still worn by Muslim pilgrims visiting Mecca during *Hajj*. His bow, of bamboo with a gut string, appears to be for hunting rather than war, and his arrows have archaic but nevertheless effective-enough stone heads. The camel's leather bridle has bronze linkage rings but there is no bit in the animal's mouth; it is controlled with a single plaited

(Left) Late Hellenistic Attic-Boeotian helmet of type today classified as 'M/G', now in the Museum für Kunst und Gewerbe at Hamburg. (Centre) Drawing of a Type G Late Hellenistic Attic-Boeotian helmet with a raised comb, from an example once in the collection of Lord Howard de Walden and today in the the Detroit Institute of Arts – see Plate F1. (Right) Variant example of Attic-Boeotian Type G.

leather rein and a stick. Nevertheless, this bedouin has acquired a simple version of the new wood-framed saddle.

H: INTERNAL TENSIONS

The Herodian dynasty ruled over a religiously and linguistically mixed part of the Middle East, where many people felt little allegiance to kings of foreign blood. A substantial part of the Jewish population similarly regarded the Herodians either as usurpers of dubious origins, or as being 'too Greek' in their culture and methods of governance. This reconstruction of a perhaps common scene in the cosmopolitan trading port of Caesarea Maritima has a Herodian *Sebastenos* cavalry trooper trying to calm a 'culture clash' between a Jewish Zealot and a Syrian woman, whose appearance reflects her people's traditional love of makeup and jewelry.

H1: *Sebastenos* cavalryman

His bronze Attic-Boeotian helmet is secured by leather thongs under the chin and around the back of the neck. His cuirass of ribbed iron scales has shoulder-pieces further strengthened by layers of rawhide; flaps of iron scales edged with leather provide extra upper arm protection, and there is an additional layer of iron scales across the upper back. The calf-length, quite tight-fitting trousers worn beneath his tunic are in a Western style, probably indicating Roman influence; the same is also true of the iron prick-spurs, with bars beneath the instep. His sword, with a horn pommel and guard and carried in a bronze-mounted scabbard, is basically the Roman cavalry *spatha*. His rather plain leather horse-harness secures an unframed but padded saddle with more thickly-padded 'horns' formed over bronze internal plates.

H2: Jewish Zealot

The simple costume worn here is based upon contemporary archaeological as well as later pictorial evidence. His religious identity is advertized by longish hair with longer side-locks. His simple open-sided tunic has the ubiquitous pair of vertical stripes, and his woollen mantle the 'notched-L' corner motifs. A crude wooden cudgel was the simplest personal weapon of civilians, also used by Roman troops to control crowds.

H3: Syrian woman

A love of personal display amongst the Syrians, both men and women, caused comment as far away as Rome, where it was wrongly regarded as a sign of moral and cultural weakness (a prejudice that long outlasted the Roman Empire). The woman in this reconstruction wears a long, almost gauzy light cotton headcloth over a bright, loosely-wound 'turban'. Her dress is relatively close-fitting, particularly in the sleeves, and is worn beneath a loose-fitting wrap secured by a large gold brooch. In addition to a large gold bracelet she has delicately-made gold pendant earrings.

INDEX

References to illustration captions are shown in **bold**. Plates are shown with page and caption locators in brackets.

Actium (naval battle) 16, 37
Agrippa I 15, 41
Agrippa II 35, 41–2
Alexander the Great 6, 9, 43, 44
Antigonus, Mattatihu 6, **6**, 10, 14, 24, 33, 34, 35, 36
Antiochus III (Seleucid ruler) 10
Antiochus IV of Syria 6
Antipater the Idumaean 6, 7, 8, 9
Antony, Marcus 8, 11, 14, 24, 34, 35, 36–7, 43
Arab tribesmen **G3**(31, 46–7)
Arbela 11, 16, 34
Archaelus 9, 12–13, 18, 41
Aretas IV, King of Nabataea 41
Aristobulus I 6, 8, 36
Aristobulus II 6
armour 8, **11**, **12**, **13**, **14**, **15**, **16**, **18**, **19**, **20**, **21**, **22**, **A2–3**(25, 43), **B1–3**(26, 43), **C2**(27, 44), **D1**, 3(28, 44–5), **E1**(29, 45), **F1**(30, 46), **H1**(32, 47), **40**, **45**
Athenion 35, 36–7
Augustus, Emperor 7, 14, 16, 35, 37, 40–1

Babylonian Jews 5, 17, 19
Batanea 7, 17, 19, 42
bodyguard troops 13, 15–16, **20**, **D3**(28, 45)

Caesar, Julius 7, 8, 15
Caesar Octavian (Augustus) 24, 35, 37
Caesarea Maritima 22, **H–H3**(31, 47), 39
camel-riders/camels **G2–3**(31, 46–7)
capes/coats/cloaks **A2**(25, 43), **C3–4**(27, 44), **D1**(28, 44–5), **F3**(30, 46)
cavalry forces 10, 11, **12**, 13, **16**, **16**, 17, 19, **20**, 21, **22**, **B3**(26, 43–4), **F1–G1**(30–1, 46), 33, 34, 35, 36, 38, 43–4
Celtic warriors 9, **15**, **15**, 21, **C2**(27, 44)
Cleopatra, Queen of Egypt 8, 16, 33, 35, 36–7
coins 6, **20**, **20**, 21, **22**, **24**, 34, **36**, 38, 39, **42**, 45

Decapolis (the) 6, 7, 36, 37
denarius (silver) 35
diadems **C1**(27, 44), **36**
dioscuri 34
doryphoroi 15, **E1**(29, 45)

equipment 20–22, **40**
  baldrics **11**, **A2**(25, 43), **B1**(26, 43), **C2**(27, 44), **G1**(31, 46)
  bowcases **B3**(26, 43–4), **F3**(30, 46)
  quivers **A1**(25, 43), **B3**(26, 43–4), **F3**(30, 46), **G2**(31, 46)
  scabbards **11**, **A2**(25, 43), **B1**(26, 43), **C2**(27, 44), **D1–3**(28, 44–5), **F3–G2**(30–1, 46), **H1**(32, 47)
  sheaths **A3**(25, 43)

First Nabataean War 10, 12, 13, 14, 15, 35–8
footwear **B1**, 3(26, 43), **C1–2**(27, 44), **D1–3**(28, 44–5), **E3**(29, 45), **F2**(30, 46)

Galatia (army) 14, **14**, 15, 16, 21, **C2**(27, 44)
Galilee 6, 7, **7**, 8, 11, 12, 19–20, 23, 24, 33–4, 42
Gallus, Aelius (Arabian expedition) 38–9
Gaul/Gauls 16, 13, **C2**(27, 44)
Gentiles 17, 19, 20, 23, 41
Germanic tribesmen (bodyguards) 9, 15, 16
Gratus (Roman commander) 13, 14, 18
guard units 14, **14**, 15, 16, 21, **C2**(27, 44), **D1**(28, 44–5)

'half-light infantrymen' **A2**(25, 43)

Hasmonaean army 13
Hasmonaean Judaea 6, **6**
Hatra (city-state), life in **D–D3**(28, 44–5)
Hatran bodyguard/envoys **D2–3**(28, 45)
headwear 8, **11**, **12**, **14**, **19**, **20**, **20**, 21, **A2–B3**(25–6, 43–4), **C2–F1**, 3(27–30, 44–6), **H1**, 3(32, 47), **34**, **40**, **42**, **43**, **44**, **46**, **47**
Hellenistic armies 3, 8, 15
Herod, King of Judaea 6
  as client king of Rome 8, 10, 35, 36–7, 38, 40
    Roman support 16, 24, 33, 34, 35, 37, 40–1
  as commander-in-chief 9, 14
    strength of bond with army 8–9, 10
  death of 9, 10, 12, 15, 41
    civil war after 14, 16, 18, 41
  depictions of **3**, **B1**(26, 43), **C1**(27, 44)
  founding of military colonies 19
  plan to relieve Masada 24, 33
  proclaimed King of Judaea 8, 9, 24, 36
  renovation of Second Temple **C**(27, 44)
  and the 'Spice Road' 36, 37, 38
  as *strategos* (military governor) 7, 8
  as unifying personality 9, 24, 33, 35, 44
Herodian army
  allegiance to Rome 3, 35
  cavalry/infantry ratio 16
  command hierarchy 10, 14
    Roman commanders 10, 12–13, 14, 18
  composition/strength of 9, 10–13, 34, 35, 36
  disintegration/division of 9, 12–13, 41
  as instrument of Herod's rule 8–10
  influences on 3, 10, 15, 16, 18, **A2**(25, 43)
  status of in Herodian state 9
Herodian kingdom/state 7, 9, 10
Herodium fortress-palace **22**, **23**, **B**(26, 43)
horse-archers **12**, 17, **17**, **B3**(26, 43–4)
horses, equipment of **B1**, 3(26, 43–4), **F1–G1**(30–1, 46), **H1**(32, 47)
Hyrcanus II, 'Ally of Rome' 6–7, 8, 9, 36

Idumaea/Idumaeans 8, 19, 34, 41, 45
  conquests of 6, 7, 11, 12, 14, 16, 33
  military colonies in 19, 20, 23
  military service 13, 14, **E1–3**(29, 45)
infantry forces 10, 11, **12**, 13, 15, 17, 18–19, **19**, 20, 21, 22, **A1**(25, 43), **B2**(26, 43), **E1–3**(29, 45), 33, 36
Ituraea/Ituraeans 7, 9, 11, 13, 17, 19, 21, 22, **A1**(25, 43), 34, 41, 43

Jericho 11, 13, 22, **22**, 33, 35
Jerusalem 5, 6, **6**, 7, 8, 9, 13, 15, 20, 22, 24, **24**, 33, 37
  siege of 10, 11, 12, 15, 24, 33, 35
Jews
  as ambassadors (murder of) 37
  antipathy towards Herodians **H**(31, 47)
  military service 9, 13, 17, 24, **A2**(25, 43), **B2**(26, 43), **F1**(30, 46), 33, 34, 38
  zealots **H2**(32, 47)
Joseph, actions in Idumaea 11, 12, 14, 16, 33, 34
Judaea 5, 6, 7, 8, 9, 18, **20**, 23, 33, 34, 35, 37, 42, 45

Machaeras (Roman commander) 11, 16, 34, 35
Masada fortress-palace 22, **33**, 45
  features/elements of **33**, **33**
  siege of 8, 24, 33, 45
mercenaries (foreign) 11, 13, 15–16, 17, **F2**(30, 46), 33
military colonies/colonists 10, 13, 19–20

Nabataea/Nabataeans 6, 9, **20**, **G**(31, 46), 34, 35, 36, 37, 38, 39–40
Nabataean army 11, 12, **22**, **G2**(31, 46), 35, 36–8, 39–40

Obodas, King of Nabataea **40**, 41
Octavian *see* Augustus, Emperor

Paleo-Hebrew inscriptions **6**
Palmyrene gods, depiction of **16**
Parthians (army) 6, 8, 11, **17**, 22, 24
Peraea 7
Phasael I 7, 8, 9
poliorcetica 14, 15
Pompey the Great 6, 7, 8, 24
Ptolemais 24, 34
Ptolemic army 10, 16, 21, 36–7
Ptolemys 5, 6

robes **C3–4**(27, 44)
Rufus (Roman commander) 13, 14, 16, 18

Sabos, King 38–9
Samaria 6, 7, 11, 12, 16, 19, 20, 23, 24, 33, 34, **34**, 35
Scythian horse-archers **17**
Sebaste (royal city) **20**, 22, 34
sebastenoi 10, 13, 14, 18, **E2**(29, 45), **H1**(31, 47), 34, 41
Second Nabataean War (9 BC) 39–41
Second Temple 5, 6, 8, **20**, **C**(27, 44)
Seleucids (army) 5, 6, 10, 16, 17, 21
shields **11**, **12**, **14**, **18**, **19**, **20**, **20**, **21**, **22**, **A2–3**(25, 43), **B2**(26, 43), **C2**(27, 44), **D1**(28, 44–5), **E1–F1**(29–30, 45–6), **G2**(31, 46), **40**, **45**
siege engines/towers/works 14, 15, 35
Silo (Roman officer) 24, 33, 34
Sosius, Caius (Roman commander) 11, 24, **24**, 34, 35
'Spice Road', fight for 35, 36, 37, 38, 39
Syllaeus (Nabataean *epitropos*) 38, 39–40, 41
Syria/Syrians 8, 24, **H3**(31, 47), 34, 40, 41, 42

Thracian mercenaries/soldiers 9, 13, 15–16, **F2**(30, 46)
Trachonitis 7, 17, 19, 39–40, 41
trousers **D1–3**(28, 44–5), **F2**(30, 46), **H1**(32, 47)
tunics **B2**(26, 43), **C1–2**(27, 44), **D2–3**(28, 45), **E3**(29, 45), **F2**(30, 46), **G1**(31, 46), **H1–2**(32, 47)

Ventidius (Roman commander) 11, 16, 24
Volumnius (Roman commander) 14, 15

war galleys 39, 42
warships (Roman) 35
weapons
  bows/composite bows 17, **17**, 21, **21**, 22, **A1**(25, 43), **B3**(26, 43–4), **F3**(30, 46), **G2–3**(31, 46–7), 39
  cudgels **H2**(31, 47)
  daggers **A3**(25, 43)
  double-edged axes 39
  javelins 21, 22, **A2–3**(25, 43), **F2**(30, 46), **G1–2**(31, 46)
  lances 22
  slings 39
  spears **18**, 21, **A2**(25, 43), **E2**(29, 45), 39
  swords **11**, **12**, **14**, **15**, **16**, **17**, **18**, **19**, **21**, **22**, **A2–B2**(25–6, 43), **C2**(27, 44), **D1–3**(28, 44–5), **F2**(30, 46), **G1–2**(31, 46), **H1**(32, 47), **40**
wraps **G3**(31, 46–7), **H3**(31, 47)

Zamaris 17, 19, **B3**(26, 43–4), 46